COTTAGE STYLE

MARY WYNN RYAN

Publications International, Ltd.

Mary Wynn Ryan is the author of *The Ultimate Kitchen* and *The Ultimate Bath* and has written about home furnishings and interior design for numerous magazines. She has served as Midwest editor of *Design Times* magazine and was director of consumer and trade marketing for the Chicago Merchandise Mart's residential design center. She is president of Winning Ways Marketing, an editorial and marketing consulting firm that specializes in home design and decorating.

Rose Sampler quilt, featured on page 52, reprinted with permission by C&T Publishing from *Hand Appliqué with Alex Anderson* (2001).

All effort has been made to feature current products on the market. However, some products may not be available from a manufacturer or retailer after the publication date. Therefore, the product information depicted in this publication is presented only as a representation of the types of products available from a given commercial or manufacturing source.

Louis Weber, CEO
Publications International, Ltd.
7373 North Cicero Avenue
Lincolnwood, Illinois 60712

Permission is never granted for commercial purposes.

Manufactured in China.

8 7 6 5 4 3 2 1

ISBN-13: 978-0-7853-5681-3
ISBN-10: 0-7853-5681-9

Library of Congress Control Number: 2001095715

Contents

Cultivating the Cottage Spirit ✎ 4

The casual, lighthearted feel of cottage style can be found in many different design schemes, including beach, vintage, and garden styles, to name just a few. Get a taste of each of these looks in this introductory chapter.

Fresh and Breezy ✎ 8

If your home doesn't have an ocean view, don't despair: The waterfront cottage look can be achieved just as easily in a city apartment as in a Malibu beach house. See the keys to creating this look in the inspiring photo spreads of this chapter.

Vintage Treasures ✎ 30

The comfy, cozy spaces featured in this chapter are sure to stir up memories of Grandma's house. Today's version of nostalgic cottage style, however, is simply warm and inviting, not fussy. Browse these pages for examples of how to mix old and new for a look that stands the test of time.

Rustic Romance ✎ 54

The rustic look may be a bit more masculine than other cottage styles, but its abundance of snug, warm wood tones appeals to both genders. This scheme works well in a brick bungalow, a log cabin in the woods, and anyplace in between, as exhibited in the homes of this chapter.

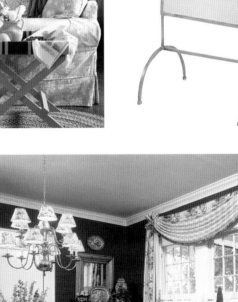

Old World Charm ✎ 80

Magical touches abound in this chapter, which highlights the many styles inspired by Europe, including English, French, Tuscan, and Swedish country. The fairy-tale-like spaces featured are sure to bring out your romantic side.

Garden Delights ✎ 104

See examples of how to bring the outdoors in with style and simplicity in the refreshing spaces of this chapter. Outdoor furniture, trompe l'oeil ceilings, terra-cotta pots, and plenty of greenery are just a few of the modest yet pretty elements that bring this look to life.

Resource Directory ✎ 126

Cultivating the Cottage Spirit

❧

IS THIS YOU? You're intuitive and creative, seeing connections others may miss. You're romantic, not just about love but about all the possibilities life offers. You're casual and spontaneous: Nobody has to remind you to seize and savor the marvels of every day.

You treasure memories of the past, but you combine mementos in your own clever, whimsical way. You're enthralled by nature, not just for its calendar-worthy splendors but for its beguiling, hidden charms. And, while you love the great outdoors, you're just as fond of a little pampering and elegance. You embrace both the sweet and the offbeat—preferably together—and the result is a deliciously lighthearted mix.

If this is you, cottage style may be, too.

Cottage style is light and spontaneous—never formal, cutting-edge, or intimidating. It's cozy without inducing cabin fever, breezy without being cold, and relaxed without being indifferent. Cottage style celebrates beautiful things and mellowed patina but in a rather offhand way. Its elegance is easygoing, and it rejects anything rigid, conformist, or self-conscious. So don't fret if your budget says no to a suite of perfectly matched or perfectly restored furniture. Cottage style thrives on the precious find mixed in with humble hand-me-downs, the fabulously old piece, and the one that's just a bit older than you are. Feel free to mix things up a bit!

ENCHANTED ELEMENTS

To capture the cottage spirit, let yourself be captivated by the relaxing charm of the imperfect and the unpretentious. Cottage style says don't store Grandma's sterling silver; use it, and fill in missing pieces with nicely made silver plate from a local flea market. Cottage style says skip that mirror with the shiny new gold-tone frame and reach for the funky painted metal one—or the one with the real gilding half rubbed off by time. Above all, cottage style says home is your personal haven, your vacation spot on the run. So relax!

Cottage style is fresh white curtains and elaborate old birdhouses, cozy wicker chairs and rusted iron bedsteads, funky pottery and graceful china. It's bead-board walls and Gothic Revival gingerbread trim, 1940s tablecloths and vintage lace, faded chintzes and rumpled white linen. Stepping into a cottage-style room, you may sense that something magical happened here that lingers still—or perhaps is just about to happen. No wonder the notion of an enchanted cottage is an image we never truly outgrow.

Around the world, cottage style appears in many guises, but it's always casually charming and undeniably romantic. Chintz-strewn English cottages and provincial French houses, rus-

The vintage cottage look wouldn't be complete without an antique quilt covering the bed. This room doesn't stop there, however: A beautiful antiqued armoire straight out of Grandma's bedroom plus lots of pretty floral accents add to the charm. Furniture designers and manufacturers: Bart and Linda Zazzali and Bart Zazzali III.

tic Tuscan dwellings and pristine Swedish homes, each have their distinctive charms. In America, cottage style reigns from northern Maine to tropical Key West and from the Pacific coast to downtown New Orleans. But what if you're not starting with an adorable little house in a scenic or historic area? Relax. The beauty of cottage style is that you can achieve the look anywhere!

ANYTIME, ANYPLACE—ANY BUDGET

Cottage style is an attitude, not an architectural type, so you can transform even a humdrum space into a delightful getaway. The icing on the cake? Cottage style is one of the easiest to pull off on a budget.

A small-scale house lends itself most readily to the look, but a bigger one can get there if rooms aren't too vast and are decorated in an unpretentious, charming way. (Think of those many-roomed "cottages" on the East Coast and the Great Lakes created for 19th-century captains of industry.) The choice is yours: Transform your whole house in cottage style, or create a cozy vacation ambience in just one or two rooms. Guest bedrooms, kids' rooms, kitchens, and garden rooms for potting and flower arranging are favorite places to create this inviting look.

SOMETHING OLD, SOMETHING NEW

Got a jumble of dark wood furniture, handed-down porch wicker, and worn gilt mirrors? Treat them to walls and fabrics in pretty tints and hot pastels to lift the look and set it free. For an even fresher feel, whitewash some of the bigger pieces, and ditch the drapes in favor of airy white curtains. Stash everyday clutter in baskets, and accessorize with things that please the *real* you.

Bring out those nostalgic old pieces you can't bear to toss, and liberate your "good" things from a life in the cupboard. A lovely old silk shawl, a rustic little birdhouse, a trio of vintage brass candlesticks, and a contemporary crystal wedding-gift bowl filled with rose petals can work charmingly together. Arrange them on a hot pink linen tablecloth for more punch: It's the element of surprise that keeps cottage style cliché-free and fresh.

One little caution: Cottage style may be a bit sentimental, but it's also chic, not country-cute. Most new retail or

craft fair accessories designed to evoke the "rustic," "country," or "beach" look miss the mark because they're contrived. True cottage style relies on the serendipity of your genuine finds: A real shell or piece of driftwood you picked up on a sunset stroll, a bird's nest your youngest found in the woods or backyard, a fragile teacup from your husband's grandmother. If you do buy accessories, look for simple, naturally styled ones—or ones so colorful and kitschy they look intentionally retro.

Blue and white is the color scheme of choice for just about any home overlooking the water. This shipshape room adds cheery yellow to the mix plus a boatload of nautical accessories to create a space that invites you aboard. Designer: Michelle Koenig.

LIGHT LOOKS

How to find the look that pulls it all together for you? In this book, you'll discover dozens of decorating schemes, all loosely grouped within five major interpretations of cottage style.

Fresh and Breezy: From California to Cape Cod and from Minnesota to Key West, waterfront cottages share sparkling views and a refreshing viewpoint. Whether permanent homes or second homes, these dwellings foster an "on vacation" spirit year-round. To support a casual indoor/outdoor lifestyle, a lighthearted, fuss-free approach is key. Vintage painted furniture from the 1920s, '30s, and '40s looks romantic and right at home here, especially if it's wicker. So do sheer or lacy white curtains, painted wood floors, and seascape accents like shells and whittled shore birds.

Vintage Treasures: Charming updates on grandmother's cottage, these homes are simply inviting—not fussy or prissy. Found in every corner of the United States (including locales as unlikely as Los Angeles), these cottages are soul-restoring havens from the clamor of modern life. New

Swedish country is a classic cottage look thanks to its cheerful yellow, blue, and white palette. Bead-board paneling and a wonderful collection of blue-and-white plates carry out the style, while a charming mix of brightly painted curvy furnishings provides a dash of whimsy. Stylist: Elaine Petrowski.

Orleans shotgun houses, Texas homes with tin roofs and dogtrots, Carpenter Gothic frame houses, tidy Cape Cods, and brick bungalows all lend themselves to this appealing look. For signature pieces, look for white iron beds, antique quilts, Depression glass, and a mix of vintage white and floral china. Relax with flea market heirlooms, such as dark, carved Victorian furniture and vintage, white-painted pieces, all set off by pastel-tinted walls.

Rustic Romance: You don't have to live in a log cabin in the woods or mountains to capture its special feeling. Log homes are obviously made for this look, but any sturdy house can create a cozy ambience. Go for old Victorian wicker, fuzzy Beacon blankets, rich-hued vintage paisley fabrics, floor lamps with funky old fringed or moccasin-laced shades, and a general air of warmth. North Woods motifs and accessories depicting moose, bears, and oak leaves are naturals here. So are Arts and Crafts— and Mission-style furnishings, as long as you don't take them too seriously as "period" styles. A popular variation, Old West style, rustles up the look with wrought-iron accessories, horse motifs, and Chief Joseph blankets.

Old World Charm: What is it about European cottage style that enchants us so? Perhaps it's the fairy tale origins or the host of wonderful associations with European cui-

Mixing tough and tender elements is a sure recipe for romance, as seen in this handsome room. Ruffles and flourishes in lush colors work just fine against the rustic wood walls and ceiling. Builder: Rocky Mountain Log Homes.

sines, literature, and gardens. Whatever the lure, there's a sense we get from European cottages that is simply magical. Choose English country if you love floral chintzes, pretty china, Bloomsbury-style pottery, and charming clutter. Look toward French and neighboring Tuscan country if you favor whitewashed stucco, richly colored mini-print fabrics, and equally colorful stoneware. Or how about crisp Swedish country, all fresh white and blue infused with sun-loving yellow? Whatever strikes your fancy, it's a village out there!

Garden Delights: Versatile and refreshing, garden cottage style can be anywhere you are. It's at home in the country or suburbs, of course, but its rejuvenating appeal is just as charming (and even more precious) in the gray of the city.

So bring teak or wrought-iron outdoor furniture inside, and use sisal and stonelike tile on the floors. Accessorize with watering cans and birdhouses, or, for a bit more elegance, use classic stone (or faux-stone) planters and elaborate bird-cages. Stencil flowering vines on the walls, and indulge in armfuls of foliage-printed fabrics and flowering plants. Paint the ceiling sky blue, hang things on trellises, and hide a realistic little majolica or cast-iron frog among the fern fronds.

Whatever cottage look appeals to you, keep it on the light side, fill in pieces as you can, and have fun with your decorating. And relax. With your own natural mix of sentiment and spirit, the enchanted cottage in your dreams can be the home you're in right now.

A rather austere room lightens up beautifully with the gentle influence of curvaceous, breezy wicker, mostly in pale colors. An abundance of live green plants and fresh-cut flowers brings the garden indoors.
Manufacturer: Lexington Home Brands.

Fresh and Breezy

MALIBU, KEY WEST, Mackinaw Island, Cape Cod...places on the water exert an irresistible lure that's like nothing else on earth. If you're lucky enough to have a water view (whether it's of an ocean or a pond), cottage style can help you make the most of it. For a wonderful beach house ambience, start with a classic seaside palette of soft blues, greens, off-whites, and beiges. Or go tropical and contrast the white with bright pastels like shrimp pink and sunset coral. Keep clutter at bay with natural rush baskets; swath comfy upholstery with crumpled white cotton duck slipcovers; paint wood floors and vintage flea-market furniture white; and hang simple white duck Roman shades (or sheers if privacy's not an issue). Bring in a few accessories to further your scheme, such as a folk-art lighthouse; a small, carved wood shore bird; an interesting piece of driftwood; and, of course, pretty shells. But keep it breezy and relaxed: The beach cottage spirit is always on vacation.

Above: *This table works overtime as a great statement of cottage style. The oval wood top is practical and visually pleasing; the rattan legs and scalloped apron lend a breezy effect.* Manufacturer: Maine Cottage.
Right: *Whitecaps and sky blue seas, white sands and deep blue lakes: The endless reverie of blue and white expresses the essence of a waterfront cottage. Painted all white for coolness and decorated with easy-care muslin, denim, and cotton, this winsome room is casually chic. Even more important, it's perfectly attuned to the sense of relaxing freedom that comes with a cottage on the water.*

A star-studded custom fixture sheds light on this roomy dining group. Cheerful red-and-white-stripe upholstered chairs make a fun and comfortable statement. Even the rug, with its compass images, carries out the nautical theme.

Star-spangled Charmer

Opposite: *Comfy roll-arm upholstery in a mix of rich red florals and blue denim balances the largely white room and hides everyday wear and tear. It's clever ideas like this that make this room easy-living as well as pretty.*

THREE CHEERS for the red, white, and blue! This nautically inspired seaside cottage pulls out all the stops, with Old Glory in a starring role. When you have a color scheme and decorative motifs this firmly in mind, shopping goes quickly. Every trip, from the mall to vacation spots, can yield more elements that fit and enrich the space. In this home, distressed painted furniture in colonial blue, cranberry red, and antique white makes a stirring color statement in every room. Simple swags add a jolt of color to windows without obscuring the wonderful views of ocean and garden. (If your view isn't quite this inspiring, translucent white pleated shades that open from the bottom up work well under swags.) If red, white, and blue isn't the look for you, choose another trio of fresh hues. Pick colors that naturally attract you, and you'll see how easily it all comes together.

Artful Expressions

A WATERFRONT HOME doesn't need a lot of complicated embellishments—not with that leading attraction just outside the window. But a great view doesn't mean a strong expression of style won't be welcome indoors. These rooms illustrate the impact of just a few important statements. Brilliant colors and dramatic (but not disturbing) artwork are just two ways to make your point without losing the relaxed summertime feeling. During the day, they add to the light-hearted fun; at night, they create drama and sparkle when the view's gone away. Just remember to keep things simple: You don't want to spend vacation weekends (or any weekends!) keeping the place pulled together. Whether your home is a bona fide seaside beauty or you just want it to feel that way, lighten your load. A few carefully chosen pieces of colorful art and comfortable furniture are all you need to warm up the place, no matter what the season.

Above: *White and neutral tones on the walls and wicker furniture make a cool canvas for some wild color plays. A long trestle table is nice for casual dining; a purple one is fabulous, day and night. Red and blue chair cushions unite in the color purple, while special paintings repeat the color scheme.* Manufacturer: Maine Cottage.

Right: *Brilliant jade green makes this bed a decorative standout in any room. While the bed would be pretty and traditional with a medley of cool blues and greens, this homeowner chose a challenging array of intense jewel tones and earth tones instead. The wall art echoes the nonconformist scheme.* Manufacturer: Maine Cottage.

A mix of blue and white with a few green notes thrown in makes a foolproof scheme for a home with a spectacular lake view. The contrast welting on the upholstered furniture and the umber-tone painting propped casually against the wall reveal an unusual attention to detail. Manufacturer: Maine Cottage.

American Holiday

BEAD-BOARD PANELING; a brick fireplace; colonial-style furniture; and a cheerful, undemanding scheme of yellow, white, and blue add up to a tried-and-true formula. What makes it fresh? The beachfront location. In a space where you might expect modern style, a traditional American scheme has an anchoring effect that's quite endearing. The only really modern elements are the big picture windows to drink in the nautical view. Added to the generous expanses of pure white, the effect is fresh, clean, and breezy. You may not have this breathtaking view, but you can adapt the overall scheme with ease. Start with simply clad or bare windows and white-painted walls, woodwork, and built-in cabinetry. Add traditional wood furniture and upholstered pieces in traditional patterns or solids. Pick up this home's yellow and cobalt blue combination, or give it a twist with aquamarine blue. Colors that celebrate sea and sky; styles that celebrate homey comforts: It's a perfect harmony!

Cadet blue and cranberry red join pristine white in this airy seaside bedroom that's just a bit on the dressy side. Wicker, rattan, and bamboo accent furniture add a slightly exotic flair to the quietly luxurious space.

Left: *With spectacular views of the ocean, this house still has a low-key, homey feeling. A classic white, blue, and yellow scheme is easy on the eyes; traditional-style furniture is comfortingly familiar; and there's a fireplace for coziness in stormy weather. What more could you ask for?* Designer: Lynn Crosby Harland, ASID, Duffy's Designs Inc.

Right: *Fresh white bead-board cabinets and sea gray granite countertops make a handsome kitchen for a waterfront home. This kitchen's sink overlooks the ocean, visible through a row of large picture windows. Your view may be more modest, but a garden pool or fountain can bring the feeling home. It's the sense, not the scale, that counts.*

Cool Running

WHAT GIVES THIS WATERSIDE HOME its witty yet comfortable air? A deft eclectic mix of American country antiques and timeless tropical pieces plus a few elegant European accents. The "shell" is just right for beachfront fun. Pretty views are left cleanly unadorned, and the floors are casual sisal and painted wood for a cool, crisp look. Color is the most compelling element in any room, and this one hits just the right note: A soothing mix of heavenly turquoise and white swaths the whole setting. Indoor and outdoor furniture mix nicely since they're all pale tones; dark accents add punch and keep the look sophisticated, never too sweet. This is one place you could happily retreat, entertain, or both—for a weekend or an endless summer.

Above: *Whether you choose sea grass, wicker, rattan, or caning, you can't go wrong with woven tropical furniture that stands the test of time. A checkerboard floor is also classic; here, in painted wood, it's chic but a bit softer in tone.*

Left: *A delightful little Victorian rococo table chills out in white, while a humble slat-back side chair gets the star treatment in a colorful plaid with dressmaker details. Blue and white never looked fresher!*

Right: *Airy white cane, natural rattan, and walls the turquoise of a sunlit sea give this room breezy waterfront style. A distressed, antiqued blue trunk makes a perfect coffee table, and Empire-inspired accents in brilliant black add flair.* Interior designer: Luciana Samu.

Peacock chairs and rockers, all in pristine white wood and wicker, look just right on this pink-and-white confection of a Victorian cottage porch. Spacious wraparound porches like this were designed for summertime sleeping in the days before air conditioning.

Lavender, pale orchid, and turquoise make a refreshingly pretty color scheme for a Victoriana porch on Martha's Vineyard. Fleur-de-lis cutouts lend a fanciful French air; an abundance of impatiens in dark rose to palest pink and white keeps the color scheme cohesive.

Old-fashioned Romance

AFFECTIONATELY CALLED "GINGERBREAD," the elaborately curly cutout embellishments on Victorian-era cottages have never lost their appeal to the romantics among us. These spectacular examples of restored vintage cottages on country-luxe Martha's Vineyard show just how decorative gingerbread can be. But beguiling as it is, this style doesn't get by on its architecture alone. On a very down-to-earth level, rocking chairs speak the language of comfort everyone understands. (Just bring out a pillow or two for your back and you've got instant ergonomic perfection!) Add a simple sturdy table within reach of each chair to hold a pitcher of lemonade and the latest summer romance novel, and you're set for pure relaxation. If your setting isn't as postcard-pretty as you'd like, create an appealing short-range view with an abundance of simple-to-grow annuals you coax from a flat or two of inexpensive plants. The porch is one place where hanging plants will never go out of style.

Carved hearts and hanging flowers make pretty accents for an easy-living porch on the Vineyard. Carved lace frosts the roof overhang and lends a vaguely exotic look to the second floor's arched windows. The essentials? Comfy porch rockers, of course!

Welcoming Ambience

COTTAGE STYLE is at home anywhere the mood is friendly and gracious. Whether your place is on the seashore, in the French countryside, or in a pleasant American town, you can create a mood of relaxed elegance and comfortable charm. First, pick a color scheme that makes you happy: perhaps a beloved classic, such as red, white, and blue. Then think of what makes you comfortable: big, fluffy pillows to support the back; well-made upholstered pieces that stand up to lots of active use; unpretentious tables to stash books as well as serve drinks; or low-key window treatments that provide privacy without stealing the floor. Then look for charming accents, but skip the kitschy "cottage" finds in favor of simple, elegant accessories. A flowering plant, a pastoral painting, and a few pieces of porcelain are all you need. Because cottage style is nothing if it's not relaxed!

Left: *A simple poster bed draped in lots of red, white, and blue makes a comfortable nest in this first-floor bedroom. If you've got room for a loveseat, it's an easy way to transform an ordinary sleeping spot into a suite deal.*

Right: *A suburban ranch house inspired by both the sea and the French countryside expresses the best of both worlds. A white-painted brick fireplace surround is cool and casual; topiaries on the mantel and a scenic oil painting add formal notes. Fun pillows and pretty, comfortable seating are especially inviting.*

Whitewashed floors and white walls and furniture could be too much of a good thing but not with the punch of brilliant peacock blue. A few bright blue decorative accessories and artworks join a pair of sleek upholstered dining chairs in the same color to really wake up the room. Manufacturer: Maine Cottage.

Bedazzling in Blue

FOR A FOOLPROOF, refreshing scheme, think blue plus white. Whether your taste is classical, country, or contemporary, blue and white can bring your style to life. The most famous blue-and-white duos pair a midrange blue with true white or antique white. But if one hue doesn't do it for you, why not follow the lead of these homeowners and use a range of related tints based in blue? Analogous color schemes are naturally harmonious but provide more visual variety than a one-color look. Take the scheme of violet, blue-violet, blue, blue-green, and green: It's cool, contemporary, and lively without being strident, so it works in bedrooms as well as more public spaces. For a livelier look, you might choose the range of blue, blue-green, green, yellow-green, and yellow. You get the idea. For maximum impact, surround the colors with lots of white; for a more subtle effect, choose beige or another neutral. With blue, you've got it made in the shade.

Above: *A pretty, traditional dresser and mirror take on a contemporary air against a colorfully striped background. This is no ordinary stripe, however. Each alternating row blends from blue to green, and the white stripes between recall the chinked walls of log cabins.* Manufacturer: Maine Cottage.

Right: *Bunking with pals or siblings in a vacation home is one of the simple joys of summer. This room could easily translate to a shared bedroom anywhere. Quaint beds in brilliant hues are personalized with different headboard cutouts and adjacent colors handpicked for lighthearted harmony.* Manufacturer: Maine Cottage.

Breezy and Beautiful

THESE ROOMS seem the stuff of fantasy, but their inviting beauty doesn't really depend on spectacular views. The fresh, graceful ambience is due mostly to the way they're furnished. Starting with an all-white shell for an expansive, simple feeling, each room includes many special (but not necessarily expensive) pieces. Let your eye tell you how to mix it up in style. Stash a casual bleached basket beneath a formal wood table to neaten a room quickly. Use white duck slipcovers you can throw in the wash after an ice cream spill, but embellish them with opulent jacquard and damask pillows. (Be sure to repeat the pillows' main colors in several other places throughout your room.) Display crystal and antique silver with some of nature's equally beautiful creations, such as seashells. The look? Cool as a sea breeze.

Left: The look of this room is elegant but not stiff because every formal element is balanced by simple, down-to-earth ones. The casual beamed ceiling and simple fireplace chimney breast, for example, lighten the look of formal furniture and ornate accessories. An 18th-century-style chest behind the sofa gets a cool and simple look with a coat of white paint.

Above: *A Chinese red table, a collection of old musical instruments with weathered red paint, and a clutch of rose-tinted pillows are all it takes to inject a lively, romantic spirit in this white room. While not the usual beach scheme, a mix of white, sand, and soft red is a sophisticated wake-up call.* **Left:** *White, beige, and periwinkle make a soothing, romantic impression in this dreamy bedroom. The subtle tone-on-tone effect is enhanced by a pretty mix of the luxurious and the rustic, such as a fine wool throw and a weathered white box of seashells.*

25

Seaside Idyll

THIS COTTAGE HAS an enviable view of the ocean, but its breezy decorating style would be at home anywhere you crave a lighthearted, casual look. Even if your nearest body of water is no more than a backyard water garden, you can create a relaxing ambience. The tried-and-true color scheme couldn't be simpler: a palette of seafoam blues and greens (verdigris copper is a special way to get that great turquoise tone) plus lots of white. Add bead-board paneling, a mix of traditional wood and wicker furniture all unified by white paint, and a few sentimental accents that mean a lot to you. The whole point of cottage style is relaxing with the things and people you love around you. If you can hear the ocean, so much the better.

A medley of deep violet-blue, navy, and true blue gives this simple bedroom seashore style. A comfortable chair, a cozy throw to curl up under, a blue spatterware pitcher of fresh garden blooms, and a few great old classics to read over and over again are just what you need to get away from it all.

Above: *A colonial gateleg table offers lots of extra dining space when needed without taking up too much room the rest of the time. Painted white, it's a nice companion to a mix of other white pieces in wood and wicker. In this context, a gilt mirror and rustic birdhouses look at home together on the mantel.* Architect: Mark Hutker & Associates.

Opposite: *Periwinkle blue shutters and white trim adorn a seaside cottage shingled in cedar shakes now weathered to a soft gray. A sunny cottage garden flanks the broad walk made of blue-gray slate flagstones. A look this harmonious seems effortless but is really well thought out.*

Cool and Spirited

THE SEA AIR does the same thing to possessions that time does: It weathers and ages them. So when outfitting your waterfront-inspired cottage, look for pieces with distressed, worn finishes and colors faded to soft watercolor tints. If you prefer a crisper look for your home, that's fine, too. Bright white and flag blue is a never-fail scheme with timeless, nautical inspirations. Look for the combination in sailcloth canvas, cotton duck, and crisp cotton chintz fabrics. Furniture of white-painted pine, perhaps with tops of marine-finished teak, are easygoing favorites, and wicker and rattan create an open look that's light in scale. And don't forget the very best of those seashells and pieces of driftwood you've collected over the years. They'll find a perfect home in your cottage by the sea.

This chair and ottoman in a strong modern style get a softening touch with frames covered in neutral-colored woven rope. It's an inspired choice for a beachfront cottage. Manufacturer: The Wicker Works. Architect: Thayer Hopkins.

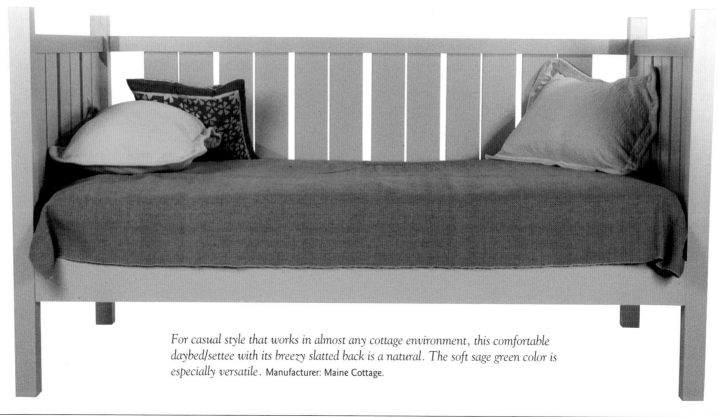

For casual style that works in almost any cottage environment, this comfortable daybed/settee with its breezy slatted back is a natural. The soft sage green color is especially versatile. Manufacturer: Maine Cottage.

Antique white glaze on a honey-finished rattan occasional table creates a mellow cottage look with a slightly tropical air. With its practical drawer and lower shelf for extra display and storage, it's great as a nightstand or an end table. Table: Laura Ashley Home. Manufacturer: Whitecraft Rattan Inc.

A vintage-style desk with a distressed finish in a soft sage green snuggles unobtrusively into just about any cottage corner. A matching chair with a woven cane seat insert makes a cool companion. Desk: Laura Ashley Home. Manufacturer: Whitecraft Rattan Inc.

A scalloped apron and big round knobs lend storybook charm to this little lingerie chest, painted a delicate powder blue. Like all good cottage-style pieces, its small scale lets it fit in just about anywhere. Manufacturer: Maine Cottage.

Comfort comes first in beach cottage style, but great design isn't far behind in this easy-living sofa. It's made of wicker over a rattan frame with wicker accents and leather bindings. Classic neutral stripes enhance the beachfront appeal. Manufacturer: Ficks Reed.

Vintage Treasures

WHEN MODERN LIFE gets complicated and isolating, our hearts go home to the nostalgic cottage style where Grandmother's cookies and a pot of tea are always waiting. Today's version of that gently reassuring style retains all the warmth without the fussiness. It's hospitable and inviting but much more relaxed than folks would have dared to be in the olden days! To create this look with fresh simplicity, skip the excess collectibles, and keep the curl-up comforts. Look for white lace curtains, voluptuous upholstered pieces made even cozier with vintage quilts, old Victorian accent pieces, white iron or old brass beds, white cutwork and cross-stitched table runners, old silver, and floral china. An old wicker picnic hamper or lidded sewing basket works nicely to hide everyday clutter. Add a copper teakettle, embroidered toss pillows, and a pretty woven afghan, and you're all settled in. Feel free to create nostalgic cottage style wherever you are, even in a city apartment. Let its comforts remind you that home really is where the heart is.

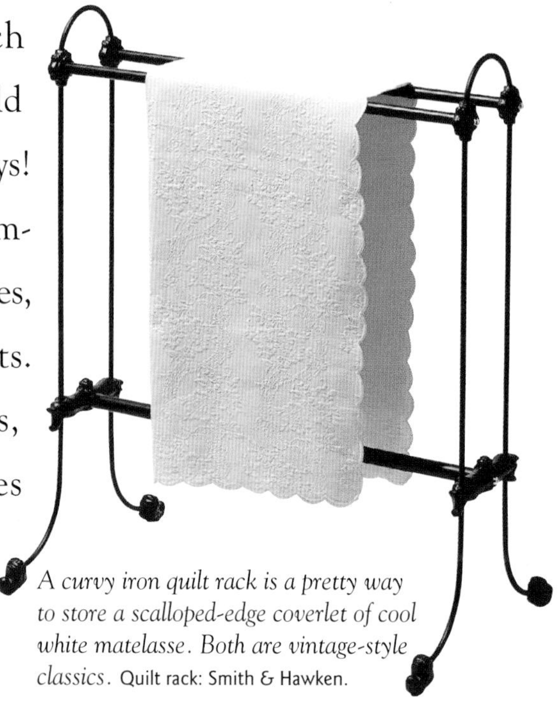

A curvy iron quilt rack is a pretty way to store a scalloped-edge coverlet of cool white matelasse. Both are vintage-style classics. Quilt rack: Smith & Hawken.

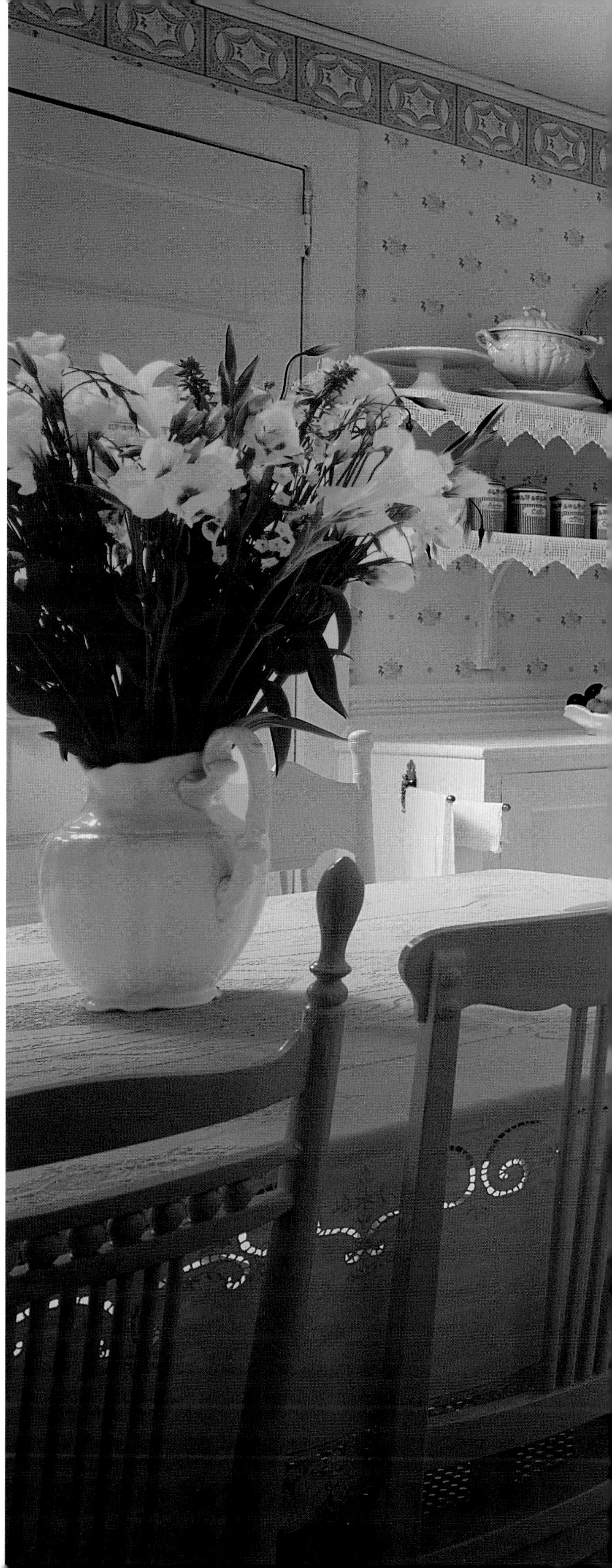

Sentimental journey: This pretty room manages to be both cool and inviting. The vintage ice box is a real treasure, but the rest of the old-fashioned elements—the white cutwork tablecloth; unmatched, white-painted Victorian chairs; and lacy scalloped shelf trim—would be practical additions to any nostalgic cottage-style space. Designer: Lyn Peterson, Motif Designs.

Flowery Bower

THE COMFORTING CHARM of these pretty retreats harkens back to a time somewhere between the Victorian era and the 1940s. The furniture and fabrics are drawn from a variety of periods, and the mix is obviously a successful one. Who wouldn't want to visit with friends in this cool yet congenial living room or sneak off for a sybaritic nap in the bedroom? To create the look of these rooms, keep the backgrounds simple and emphasize overscale, comfortable furniture. Add a few accent pieces to fill in and create visual interest. Layer on the history and charm with decorative accessories chosen because they have personal meaning or enhance a pretty color scheme. (In this living room, a collection of 1930s pottery and '40s fabrics meets both criteria.) Flea market shopping can be addictive, but to really inspire relaxation, don't let clutter take over. You want to enjoy your rooms—not spend hours dusting them!

A stenciled floor, painted wood paneling, and a host of flower-motif decorative accents give this room a breezy, garden-inspired appeal. Outside the bedroom, a vintage dresser like this would be charming in an entry hall to show off collectibles. Interior designers: Mike and Meri Hern.

Opposite: *The old rule of designing on a budget, "use inexpensive fabrics lavishly not skimpily," is obviously in play here. Simple cotton fabrics in white and ticking stripe make a great background for showing off '30s-era pottery and pillows covered in vintage tablecloths.* Interior designer: Patsy Bruce.

The 1920s and '30s saw comfy quilts and bedspreads take on fresh pastel colors from the garden and candy box. This cotton quilt in a refreshing mint tone looks surprisingly contemporary, but the white lace and flowery wallpaper are old-time favorites. Interior designer: Patsy Bruce.

A coddling cottage boudoir needs little more than good reading light, a comfortable pillow-plumped bed, and a bed table to facilitate breakfast and letter-writing. The ivory, green, and rose scheme, pretty in its own right, is given a more casual cottage air with the addition of a contrasting blue-print fabric.

Flowers and Flourishes

IF YOUR TASTE tends toward a bit more opulence than the typical cottage offers, take heart: Occasional elegant, formal touches can take a rather rustic "shell" into a dressier realm. By the same token, a few whimsical, casual touches are all it takes to loosen up a traditional look. It's up to you! Use lavish draperies, bed hangings, tablecloths, and upholstery fabrics to make a pampering statement while indulging your love of color and pattern. A more restrained combination of fabrics is more formal; frequent mixing denotes a more casual air. Magnify the appeal of special fabrics with hand-painted details on woodwork, walls, furniture, or even the ceiling. Add colorful accents, from plump chair pillows to pretty dishes, that underscore your hospitable side. Because, elegant or rustic, cottage style is always inviting.

Opposite: *Confection pink walls and green bishop's-sleeve draperies topped with pastel plaid taffeta give a rather formal setting the relaxed prettiness of a garden. Instead of the expected still life, this fireplace wall sports a painting of hydrangea in a simple terra-cotta pot. The scene painted on the mantel adds fairy tale charm.* Interior designer: Ann Platz. Ann Platz & Co.

Dramatic Simplicity

THESE ROOMS are furnished with important vintage pieces, but their overall presence is sophisticated, almost contemporary. Rigorous editing has pruned away all second-tier clutter, leaving plenty of room to appreciate the handsome shapes and textures of the essentials that remain. There's an inherently graceful quality about rooms furnished with this philosophy— a quality that is timelessly chic. For small, cottage-style rooms, there's an extra bonus to this uncluttered decorating approach: Rooms just naturally look more spacious. To get the look, start with white or interestingly tinted walls in such colors as celadon, peach, periwinkle, or parchment. Keep window treatments and floor coverings simple unless they qualify as stunning focal points in their own right. Do the same with furniture and lighting fixtures. As for accessories, they don't have to be expensive or even true antiques as long as they're remarkable—and genuinely "you"!

Above: *This old iron bed with folk-art cutouts might look corny in a more cluttered context. In this clean-cut setting, it's simply whimsical. "Simply" is key: There's ample space around each element in the room so you can appreciate the interesting lines of each piece. The cool, quiet color scheme furthers the soothing mood.*
Left: *A few vintage finds—in this case, lamp finials and dollhouse furniture—make unique accessories to ornament this simple antique desk. Taken with the framed floral print and pair of diminutive lamps, the assembly makes for a charming vignette. Group your finds similarly for decorative impact.*

A beautifully shaped loose-pillow sofa, a grandly scaled mirror, a richly colored rug, and a big old coffee table with a mottled finish: They're all useful elements, but, more than that, they all have great presence. Simple? Yes. Sparse, cold, or skimpy? No way! Interior designer: Jeannie Oberholtzer.

A luxurious mix of fabrics from bright white to rich rose gives this vintage-style bedroom a lively, romantic feeling. If you've collected or inherited a rich variety of antique finds in dark, aged colors like these, give them added importance and a visual lift from the fresh backgrounds.

Scattered roses in pale pink and deep red tones enliven a vintage-style bath. Pale pink terra-cotta floor tiles blend right in, and old plaster walls in palest green wrap it all together. Furniture and accessories: Spiegel.

Rose in Bloom

Opposite: *Vintage English cottage style comes to life with tea-stained or other antique-looking fabrics. This scheme adds pretty accents of rich rose, green, and off-white.* Manufacturer: Sanderson.

SOFTER, LESS OBVIOUS, and more interesting than fire engine red, rose red is a heart-warming color few can resist. Akin to rich cranberry and sophisticated wine tones, rose is a natural with off-white, taupe, or beige in a vintage decorating scheme. There's no more romantic look, especially if you like English country style or one of its offshoots. Rose is flattering in a bedroom or bath, hospitable in a dining room or living room, and just plain inviting anywhere. The adventurous decorator might apply rose full strength onto walls, but as these three rooms show, just a little rose goes a long way. Walls can be just about any color, but soft green and pale pink are proven winners. Strew some rose tones on small upholstered furniture pieces, throws or pillows, and lamp shades and other accent items throughout the room. And don't forget a bouquet or two of the real thing!

Robust Romantic

THE LATE 18TH-CENTURY ROMANTICS were in love with an idealized vision of nature as well as with love itself, a perspective that has never completely gone out of style. This cottage celebrates the romantic spirit from floor to ceiling and everywhere in between. Knotty pine walls, most often seen in much more rustic homes, make a rich, unusual background for a wealth of delicate details. It's this unique mix that makes the look so romantic. Lace, floral, and toile fabrics; pale-tinted botanical prints; and lots of china and gilt could become oppressive, but not against this background. Instead, the rough wood creates a bracing effect and shows that the owners, while at home with elegance, don't take themselves too seriously. The result? A space that breaks the rules but is warmly indulgent all the same.

Luxurious but not at all stiff, this knotty pine room has an unusually opulent air thanks to richly patterned fabrics and a wealth of gilt and china accents. Prettily framed family photos lend a casual and sentimental feeling that's very much in the cottage spirit.

A riot of lace, toile, leopard, and floral fabrics gets a refreshingly tailored, casual touch from a ticking-stripe dust ruffle and a homespun patchwork quilt in—what else?—the traditional double wedding ring pattern. Fine antique furniture looks offhandedly mellow next to rustic knotty pine walls.

Opposite: *A vintage dressing table swathed in rose-print fabric and accented by an extravagantly carved wood mirror makes a romantic focal point. The impression is one of many prints, but, in reality, all's been deftly planned: Each fabric appears at least twice. The lettuce green ceiling is just one more fearless touch.*
Interior designer: Ann Platz, Ann Platz & Co.

Relaxing Charm

WHETHER IT'S A REAL MEMORY or just a wishful reverie, almost everyone has a place where, as the poet put it, you know you're home because they have to take you in. If you don't have a grandmotherly type waiting in the wings, take heart: Creating this kind of cottage space for yourself is easier than you may think. Start with vintage fabrics—especially tablecloths, kitchen towels, and bed linens—from resale shops. Choose comfortable upholstered pieces and freshen them up with loose-fitting, pale slipcovers. Fill in with a mix of wicker and distressed wood furniture: generously sized coffee tables; charming accent pieces; and, of course, a comfy rocking chair. So what if your cookies are the slice-and-bake variety? This home offers comfort that's straight from the heart.

Above: *An antique cupboard and mirror, their original white finish crackled with age, would make an interesting focal point in any room. Converted into a vanity for this otherwise up-to-date bath, they're spectacular.*

Opposite: *This home conjures up an indulgent grandma who's always glad to see you. Loose-fitting slipcovers, distressed white wood and wicker furniture, and vintage flowery fabrics add up to a room with quintessential cottage style.* Interior designer: Simple Slips.

Vintage floral fabrics from the 1930s and '40s give a nostalgic boost to this snuggly retreat. A graceful sleigh bed piled with white-and-rose pillows is especially pretty next to celestial blue walls. Small wonder the painting's angel looks right at home.

43

How delicious to curl up in a pretty boudoir like this! A white-painted wrought-iron bed and hand-decorated farm chest are romantic essentials. Custom stained glass, now enjoying renewed popularity, is great for enhancing privacy without blocking light.

Welcoming Cheer

BACK IN THE DECADES just before and after World War II, homes all over America looked a lot like these friendly rooms. Simple, pretty, comfortable, and clean, they welcomed families big and small. Both sentimental and retro chic, the unfailing charm of this nostalgic style is used to full effect here. Because this 1940s-era house has not yet undergone much modern renovation, the homeowners wisely sought out vintage accents, from glass drawer pulls in the kitchen to dresser scarves for the bedroom's farm chest. (Original versions of these elements can still be found in resale shops, but their popularity has also made them available as reproductions through stores and catalogs.) Enhancing the simple, cheery look, each room shares the primary color scheme of red, yellow, and blue. Lots of white visually expands the rooms and gives them an especially clean, fresh ambience. Grandma would be proud.

Opposite: Old-fashioned charm abounds in this welcoming kitchen dressed in cheerful primary colors plus lots of white. Inspired by kitchens of the 1930s and '40s, it's lovingly decorated with family hand-me-down favorites and flea-market finds.
Interior designer: Kay Dande.

An open shelving unit recalling Welsh dressers of old is painted buttercup yellow to match the wood-work. A big part of this room's natural charm is the wallcovering borders and coordinating fabric featuring realistically colored pansies.

Blithe Spirit

Blue skies and sunshine yellow, a lot of white, and a bit of bright red—this simple formula never fails to raise spirits. And there's no better way to express cottage style at its cheeriest! These rooms owe much to the inspiration of Victorian grandmamas who confidently mixed many prints as long as they were in the same color scheme. Also Victorian is additional layering with an abundance of knickknacks. The lighthearted color scheme, however, is much more here and now. With a youthful palette made up of the three primary colors (clear red, yellow, and blue), even a very traditional setting gets a contemporary kick. You could create a different but equally fresh effect with hot pastel versions of the three secondary colors (green, lilac, and peach). For best effect, choose one color to dominate, another to play second fiddle, and the third to appear as an accent. Keep it light with lots of white.

Opposite: *When the front door opens right into the living room, you know you're in a classic cottage. There are more than half a dozen different prints in this elegant little parlor, but they all work. Almost every-thing stays true to the color scheme of golden yellow, white, and royal blue.*
Interior designer: Debi Allison.

Nostalgic Elegance

THERE'S SOMETHING almost dreamlike about these rooms, and therein lies their timeless charm. They're a mélange of archetypal images that evoke bygone comforts (or, at least, what we would like to believe were true of the good old days). In fact, these rooms are much cooler, cleaner, and brighter than they would have been way back when. But the graciousness and simple pleasures they recall are just as appealing as ever. Comfortable beds with lots of pillows and cushy chairs for sharing conversation with friends and family: What more could a dreamer want? To get the look, choose old (or vintage-style) furniture; paint it white; add lots of white and tea-stained fabrics; and embellish with pretty, old-fashioned accessories that are also useful, such as creamware pitchers and graceful little tables. Grandmother would approve.

Opposite: *Vintage floral and solid-color fabrics in soft, muted tones all blend beautifully together. In contrast, the walls, striped in sprightly periwinkle and white, add a strong, fresh touch that gives the whole room a very confident, whimsical look.* Furnishings: Spiegel. Above right: *Like pretty sisters, unmatched but similar in charm, these white-painted twin beds are a cool and welcome place to curl up on a summer's evening. The pretty, layered effect is easy to create: Just buy two sets of bed linens and mix them up.* Furnishings: Spiegel.

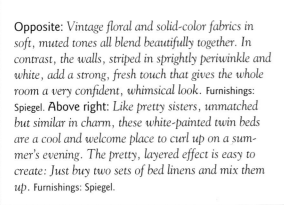

Old needlework and pictures, nicely framed, make evocative art for a nostalgic cottage bedroom. The bed, dressed in a mix of crisp white cutwork and jewel-tone needlepoint, is comfortable and pretty. In sentimental cottage style, an old door, its ancient paint heavily crazed with age, makes a poignant backdrop for a frothy organza christening gown.

Sentimental Journey

THESE ROOMS are all furnished differently, with varying color schemes and furniture styles. But all share a nostalgic, homespun charm that's hard to beat. Hoop-back Windsor chairs; wicker and rattan porch furniture; and distressed, painted pieces of all kinds have stood the test of time. Used together or separately, they mix nicely in a way that is almost as effortless as it looks. Old things with humble, useful origins, chosen for their unassuming beauty and timeworn charm, find new life as objets d'art. The nice thing about this decorating style is that you can probably find a lot of the elements in your grandmother's attic, your local resale shop, or a regional antique fair. Other elements have attained classic status, so they're being reproduced by today's manufacturers of everything from dining tables to quilts. Old or just old-looking, these are the pieces that bring back sweet memories of home.

Above: *Before air conditioning enticed everyone indoors for the summer, a screened porch and airy wicker furniture were the coolest things in town. On this porch, a collection of birdhouses, a vintage trellis, and an old garden gate keep company with unpretentious seating. Pass the lemonade!*

Opposite: *An imposing corner cabinet/ armoire and a generously sized dining table gain added eye appeal from their weathered, painted finishes in shades of aqua and true blue. Aqua-painted baskets and a sky blue quilt, once functional, are treated as the decorative treasures they also are.* Interior designer: Harvestings.

Made for Memories

WHETHER YOU FERRET OUT the best from the family attic or haunt the most interesting flea markets in your area, you'll find that vintage style is one of the easiest to recreate. And while the last several decades have seen a new appreciation for vintage finds (and appreciated prices to match), there are still lots of wonderful old pieces around. Vintage style can be charmingly sentimental or downright funky. Pastel-colored cotton quilts, lace-edged bed linens, and colorful and fruit-printed cotton fabrics provide a coddling sense of coziness. For furniture, vintage wicker and rattan mix nicely with painted old pine armoires and lovingly preserved mahogany tea tables. (Beds are one place you may prefer a reproduction, as today's beds are bigger and cribs are safer.) Indulge in pastel-tinted Depression glass, funky 1930s kitchenware, and other artifacts from Grandma's era. They're sweet and sturdy—just like the good ol' days.

A spacious armoire, originally used to house arms in medieval France, stashes everything these days from bed linens to home electronics. A distressed white finish keeps a big piece like this from dominating the room, while bull-nose and reeded column details add a classic touch. Armoire: Ballard Designs.

Floral quilts added artistry, color, and warmth—both visual and physical— to rustic cottage homes for generations and were commonly made through the 1930s in rural America. Today, antique and vintage quilts are perfect as wall art, and reproductions make classic patterns practical for everyday use. Designer: Alex Anderson.

Whether it's a real hand-carved wood antique with genuine gold gilding or a budget-friendly molded resin look-alike with faux gilt, you'll want at least one or two pretty mirrors in your cottage-style room. Choose one with a built-in candleholder to double the romantic light in the space. Manufacturer: Swedish Blonde.

Depression glass added delicate color and sparkle to homes in the 1930s. Highly collectible today, the heavily detailed glass comes in pale pink and various other tints. Dessert services, candlesticks, punch cups, and entertaining accessories are most prevalent and mix nicely with vintage white floral china.

Designed to fit in even the coziest cottage spaces, this flip-top table is stylish and practical, thanks to clean lines and durable metal corners. Matching wooden chairs evoke the feeling of an Italian bistro, while the distressed white finish turns an ordinary table set into a vintage treasure. Table and chairs: Ballard Designs.

For old-fashioned charm and sentiment, you can't beat an inviting chair like this one. A ruffled skirt and roll arms offer pretty comfort; contrast-print arm ends add verve. A coordinating pillow is a valentine to vintage style. Manufacturer: Della Vita.

Evoking images of bygone romance, this hand-cast iron bed wears a weathered white finish. An urn of fruits flanked by birds makes a charming motif for the headboard. Bed: French Country Living.

Rustic Romance

Y OU DON'T HAVE TO BE the outdoorsy type to enjoy the warmth of a campfire, the coolness of a mountain brook, or the appeal of time-less rustic style. Modern lifestyles long for the nourishing connection to forests and mountains, and home is the perfect place to indulge this desire. While the beachfront cottage look is fresh, breezy, and out in the open, rustic cottage style is an embracing haven, as deliciously cozy as a tree house retreat or a frontier cabin. If you don't have a real log cabin, a brick bungalow or any snug den will do. Create a year-round vacation hideaway with a casual mix of log furniture, Victorian mahogany accents, 1930s wicker rocking chairs, Arts and Crafts– and Mission-style furnishings, funky vintage lamps, and blankets in warm tones. Borrow a few deer and fir tree motifs for a North Woods look, add more ferns and leaping salmon to take the look into the Great Northwest, or use horse and Native American motifs to evoke the Old West. Don't overdo it, though; rustic style is never cute, always hearty and authentic.

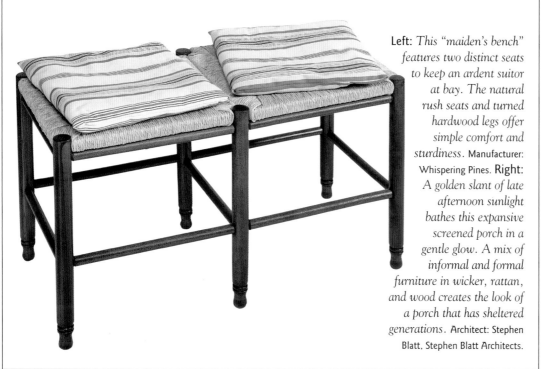

Left: This "maiden's bench" features two distinct seats to keep an ardent suitor at bay. The natural rush seats and turned hardwood legs offer simple comfort and sturdiness. Manufacturer: Whispering Pines. Right: A golden slant of late afternoon sunlight bathes this expansive screened porch in a gentle glow. A mix of informal and formal furniture in wicker, rattan, and wood creates the look of a porch that has sheltered generations. Architect: Stephen Blatt. Stephen Blatt Architects.

Woodland Hideaway

OVERLOOKING A LARGE LAKE from its forest vantage point, this home is undeniably spectacular. But even if your best view is only of your own backyard, there's no reason why you can't make the most of warm and charming rustic cottage style. Where most homes with this kind of architecture take a modern turn or one that's lumberjack-rustic, this house celebrates a more romantic, timeless look. With good-size windows, midtone pine paneling like this doesn't become oppressive. A charming mix of dark-painted wicker, Mission-style accents, and cushy upholstered pieces gives this space an unusually sophisticated, lighthearted ambience. Piling on the riot of colorful unmatched but coordinating pillows helps give the space a lavish look you wouldn't quite expect in a pioneer-inspired setting. Plenty of fresh flowers echo the charming rock-garden ambience and pick up the rosy pink tones of the pillows and throws. This is a room that would be just as inviting in suburbia as in a mountain glen.

Opposite: *Not every house can have the soaring views and savvy architecture of this space, but anyone can bring a rustic vacation ambience home. Colorful jewel-tone fabrics inspired by Provence and dark-painted wicker furniture are what make this home so inviting.* Architect: Bernhard & Priestley Architecture LLC.
Right: *A woodland eyrie snuggles unobtrusively among the trees overlooking a serene mountain lake. You may not be able to duplicate this location, but the peeled log bed, picture windows, all-white flowering shrubs, and other quiet touches are well within reach.*

A riot of deep-tone patterns works masterfully together on this bed because they all share the red, white, and blue color scheme. Still more patterns decorate lamp shades and window valances, but the effect is simply cozy, not cluttered.

Rich and Rustic

AS A DESIGNER, this homeowner understands that a room that "just happens" is not as relaxing as one that's artfully put together. Inspired by influences as varied as a Bavarian fairy tale and a Teddy Roosevelt–style hunting lodge, this cottage in the woods exudes warmth, drama, and charm aplenty. For starters, richly colored walls, either painted or natural wood, create a cozy look. Jewel-tone fabrics layer on even more warmth and visual appeal. While many rustic homes take a strictly lumberjack-plaid approach, this one uses formal and floral accents for romantic appeal. Careful attention to balancing colors makes this a sophisticated space, too. For example, the zippy black, white, and brown pillows tie in with the mostly red, gold, and green room thanks to a painting of hunting hounds. The finishing touch? Lots of appropriately framed family photos add to the personal appeal of every room.

Opposite: *Even if you prefer nature paintings to hunting trophies, the deep-woods appeal of this room is undeniable. This is a decorating scheme that takes wonderful chances. For example, a gloriously formal roll-arm sofa in brilliant red looks right at home.* Interior designer: Ann Platz, Ann Platz & Co.

The more you look at Arts and Crafts–style furniture, the more interesting it appears. What other style is inspired by Jacobean and other medieval European designs, timeless Asian styles, and the rustic looks of primitive cultures around the world? Adding a note of natural color, celadon green pottery bridges these cultural gaps with quiet grace.

Artful Craftsmanship

WHILE WE MOST OFTEN think of cottage style as romantic and rather pretty, there are alternatives for those who prefer a more tailored effect. Inspired by classic Arts and Crafts style and by the 1930s version of that venerated design school, these bungalow rooms have a handsome, straightforward look that's timeless in its appeal. Modernists and traditionalists alike can appreciate the dignified lines and lovely handcrafting of each element in these rooms— not only the furniture but the architecture and the accessories, too. Painted white, it has a surprisingly contemporary, fresh look; stained in dark wood tones, it's dramatic without forsaking its essential simplicity. Against these austerely beautiful basics, special touches such as geometric-patterned stained glass windows and lamp shades gleam all the more brightly. Arts and Crafts style is in the midst of a great resurgence in popularity, so you can find nicely made reproductions of furniture, wallcoverings and wallpaper borders, decorative accessories, lighting fixtures, and more.

Above: *A classic kitchen nook makes a cozy breakfast area for a pair of lovebirds or a small family. The mix of white-painted wood and shiny stainless steel/chrome is lots of fun, and the vintage '30s green glass dishes carry out the charming mood.*

Left: *A great fieldstone fireplace is a stunning focal point in this bungalow living room that's an homage to Arts and Crafts style. The dark-, medium-, and light-colored leather upholstery provides just enough visual variety as well as durable comfort.*

The Royal Treatment

WHO SAYS you can't use flowers and romantic colors in a log home? With vistas of the Grand Tetons, perhaps purple mountain majesties were the inspiration. This handsome house made of lodge pole pine uses deep purple as its main accent color. It's a masterful choice, as violet is the perfect complement to the golden yellow hues of the wood. But it's not just the royal purple color that lends this home its rather romantic European ambience. Grand gestures and romantic ones abound with a confident sensibility. The most dramatic focal points are the unique fireplaces in the bedroom and living room: They combine two stones native to the Rockies, Dakota dry stack stones on the fireplace surround and river rock on the chimney breast. Fine oil paintings, English floral upholstery, antiqued furniture and cabinet woods, and lavish use of granite give this forest-inspired home a surprising yet comfortable elegance.

Above: A masterpiece of a space, this room pays homage to timeless, natural materials. Most dramatic, the vast island pairs antiqued pine cabinets and stacked slate stones beneath a mellow golden granite countertop. A ventless fireplace is the crowning touch.

Bedding in blue-violet florals and white eyelet gives a pretty, almost Alpine feeling to this log home bedroom. The sleigh bed and armoire add to the romantic European air.

Lighted oil paintings, floral upholstery, and handsome rugs laid over plain carpeted floors add levels of luxury and plush comfort. The dramatic one-of-a-kind fireplace is a fabulous focal point. Designer: Daren Martin Walsh, ASID, Silver Sage Design. Builder: Bob Moore Construction.

Woodland Fantasy

RUSTIC STYLE is usually rather squared-off, but the owners of this wonderfully expressive log home took a very different direction. Its size stretches the definition of cottage a bit, but its spirit is pure cottage enchantment. You might expect Hansel and Gretel or the Seven Dwarfs to arrive at any moment. Columns, built-ins, and decorative accents have all been treated to fantastic carvings that are fun and whimsical yet powerfully archetypal. Are the round columns carved with barber pole stripes inspired by Alaskan totem poles or temples in Bali? Is the bed niche a charming take on Swedish style, or does it evoke a Hungarian gypsy caravan? Whatever the genesis of these architectural elements, the owners have clearly stood the conventional log cottage look on its ear. The result? A home that's playful, romantic, and ageless.

Recalling the charming Scandinavian artwork of Carl Larsson, this cozy sleeping niche boasts twin beds with platform storage drawers, a nightstand/bookcase, and a canopy-effect ceiling, all wonderfully detailed with scroll carvings.

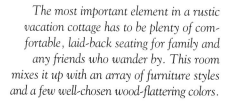

The most important element in a rustic vacation cottage has to be plenty of comfortable, laid-back seating for family and any friends who wander by. This room mixes it up with an array of furniture styles and a few well-chosen wood-flattering colors.

Mountain Greenery

A RUSTIC HOME made of vintage barn boards is undeniably handsome, but sweetly cheerful furnishings are what make it so livable. In this home, a simple, natural palette of white and light green sets off dark-hued aged wood to perfection. Even more important, it keeps the space from looking overwhelming. Thanks to the visual relief of generous amounts of white and green (plus a few shots of just-for-fun clear colors), this space is anything but oppressive. Instead, its spirit is light-hearted, inviting, family-friendly, and romantic. The beauty is that you can replicate this cottage look in just about any space; the scale of the furniture would be just as much at home in a suburban house as in this dramatic barn. While so-called "earth tones" go in and out of style, it's hard to imagine a more soothing, grounding scheme than dark brown, light green, and white. Add a few treasures in your own favorite colors, and relax!

Pale green-and-white floral fabric lends a fresh spring-time air to this rustic home. A coordinating green lamp shade and a rainbow-colored rag rug add to the lighthearted ambience.

Opposite: *Soft sage green and white upholstery makes a pretty contrast to the darkly rustic wood walls and stone fireplace in this lodge-style home.* Furnishings: Whispering Pines.

Brilliant Aesthetic

IN AN ERA ruled by "over-the-top-ulence," some interesting definitions of elegance are being reborn. More and more often, elegance appears as a clear, clean use of ample space; furnishings that are both functional and beautiful; an appreciation for natural materials; and a passionate attention to handcrafted details. These rooms exemplify this new look, which owes a lot to the Arts and Crafts movement. There are no overdone, cluttered elements, yet there's no sense of cold austerity, either. The rooms hold what they need, and everything they hold is calculated to delight the eye and captivate the mind. To get the look, choose well-designed, well-made furniture with integral, not glued-on, decorations. Mix Asian, European, and vintage American (1730s or 1930s) pieces as long as their proportions are compatible. Rein in the clutter, and save space for a few real handcrafted treasures. Less really is more, if what there is, is great!

Above: *Simple but masterfully designed, the wood trim in this restful room creates a lovely frame for special furnishings. Slate green tiles on the fireplace surround make a subtly elegant statement, and the mantel acts as a fine showcase for vintage 1920s and '30s accessories. True to the Arts and Crafts aesthetic, the novel striped end table is a one-of-a-kind focal point that's also useful.*

Right: *From the wood-bordered tin ceiling to the custom area rug, this room abounds in wonderful Arts and Crafts inspirations. The architecture and the furnishings are completely in sync—a rare luxury in itself. On every side, the movement's Asian, medieval European, and Early American influences are on display. The tricolored clock table is a special treasure.*

Left: *A sunroom that recalls the gently exotic look of a tropical British colony makes a delightful retreat. Comfortable roll-arm wicker seating, a masterful stone-inset floor, and a charming trompe l'oeil dresser-turned-end table are exactly what's needed.*
Builder: Castlerock Homes Inc.
Designer: Mascord Design
Associates. Interior designer:
Jayne Sanders Interior Design.

Woodland Trails

For those whose idea of a corner office includes a forest view instead of a city one, this desk on convenient casters can be tucked just about anywhere. Heightening the rustic look are bark-on chairs with funky cowboy-motif upholstery.

THE BELOVED LOG CABIN LOOK borrows from many influences. Old West style depends on woven rope, saddle leathers, horseshoes, and other cowboy motifs along with a palette of lots of gold, brown, and russet tones. North Woods style comes alive with depictions of moose, bears, and lumberjack plaids in hunter green and cranberry red. Bavarian cottage style features curvy carved gingerbread trim; fabrics with embroidered or woven mountain-meadow flowers; and a color scheme of cobalt blue, soft white, and cheery red. What's common to all: black wrought iron, unpretentious comforts, and natural wood everywhere. The house appears closest to the Old West theme, but the snowshoes over the mantle hint at North Woods style. You could turn the look easily with just a few accessories and upholstery fabrics. That's the beauty of this style: It's as versatile as it is comfortable.

With French doors over-looking the cedar deck, this dining area has built-in appeal. The wood table and chairs, embellished with hand-carved, simple decoration, encourage hearty hospitality without fuss.

Opposite: *A fieldstone fireplace and log walls are set off by furnishings in the spirit of things: leather and Native American–blanket upholstery, moccasin-laced lamp shades, and vintage accents collected through the years.* Builder: Rocky Mountain Log Homes.

A Tradition of Dignity

WHEN WE THINK OF Early American style, many think of a frontier cabin. This home's inspiration dates from the Early American era but not out on the frontier. Rather, it recalls the stately graciousness of the colonial and early Federal periods. Recycled bricks for flooring, a traditional-style armoire to hide the TV, Shaker-style hooks for coats, and an antique hope chest for a coffee table are just a few of the masterful touches that make this home resonate with vintage charm. Even the modern touches are handsomely scaled and basically simple; for example, the pair of traditional sofas treated as a sectional and upholstered in a rich orange-red that brightens the exposed-beam family room. Furniture includes both rustic country pieces and timelessly elegant ones, such as the Queen Anne wing chair. True antiques from this era are rare and costly, but, fortunately, reproductions of these beloved styles are widely available today.

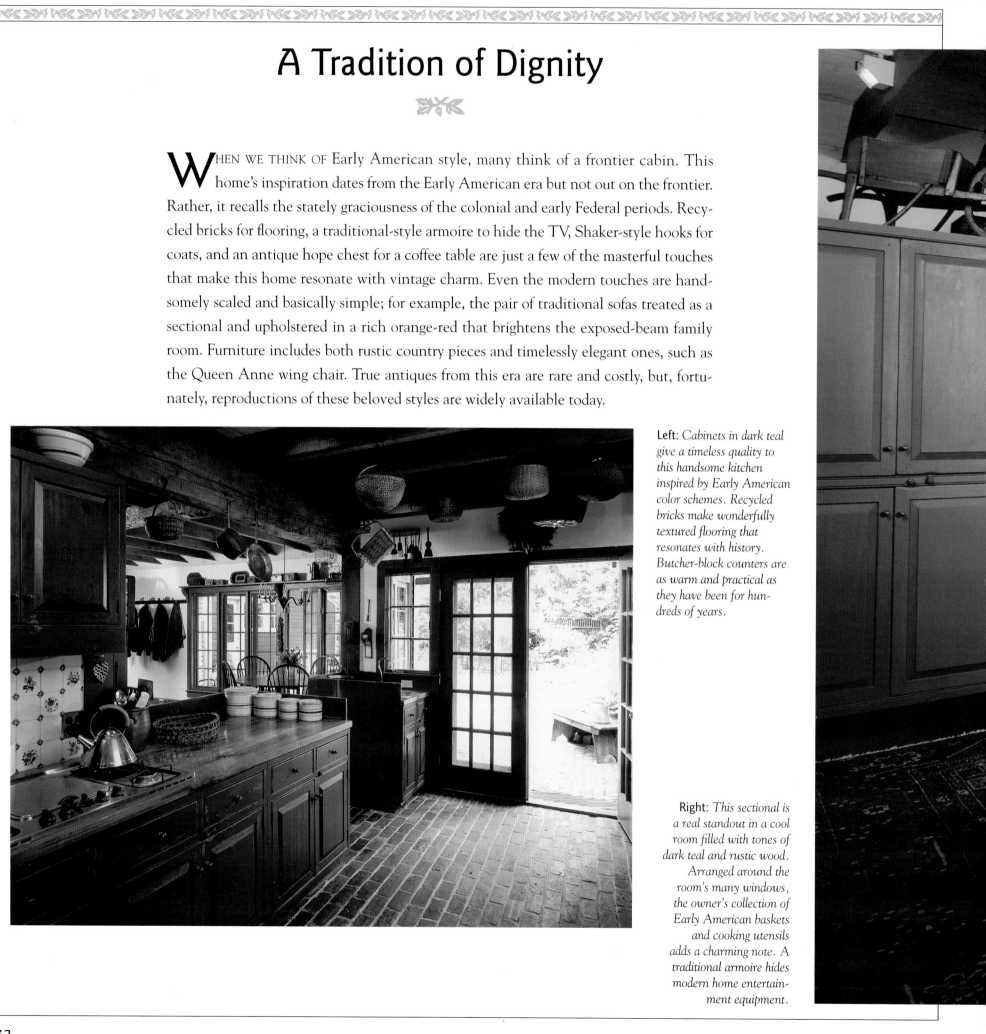

Left: *Cabinets in dark teal give a timeless quality to this handsome kitchen inspired by Early American color schemes. Recycled bricks make wonderfully textured flooring that resonates with history. Butcher-block counters are as warm and practical as they have been for hundreds of years.*

Right: *This sectional is a real standout in a cool room filled with tones of dark teal and rustic wood. Arranged around the room's many windows, the owner's collection of Early American baskets and cooking utensils adds a charming note. A traditional armoire hides modern home entertainment equipment.*

Peaceful Dignity

A plainly styled loggia, or overhead openwork structure, supports the heavy vines of orchid pink wisteria in this timeless setting. Simplicity, dignity, and appropriateness reign, and the setting recalls native architecture from many cultures around the world, from Navajo to Tuscan to Japanese. The common bond: humanly scaled homes that relate to the land.

"HAVE NOTHING IN YOUR HOME that you do not believe to be beautiful or know to be useful" was the rallying cry of the artists and architects who brought us the Arts and Crafts movement. It's still a challenging goal when it comes to furnishing and decorating the home today. Born in the 19th century, the Arts and Crafts movement was a reaction against ornate Victorian style and the Industrial Revolution, which made it possible to mechanically add meaningless decoration to furnishings of all kinds. Austere and strong, Arts and Crafts styles, including Eastlake, Stickley, and Mission, among others, influenced the later Prairie School and other 20th-century modern styles. In the last several decades, original Arts and Crafts style has had a popular renaissance. As with the solid, foursquare bungalow, Arts and Crafts style owns a permanent lock on the American heart.

Left: *Just a few carefully chosen accessories embellish this cool and dignified bungalow cottage dining room. Arts and Crafts furniture, created with the forthright bungalow in mind, looks beautifully at home. An austere scheme of linen white plus medium and dark brown wood tones looks simple, but in a minimalist setting, each element must be fine.*

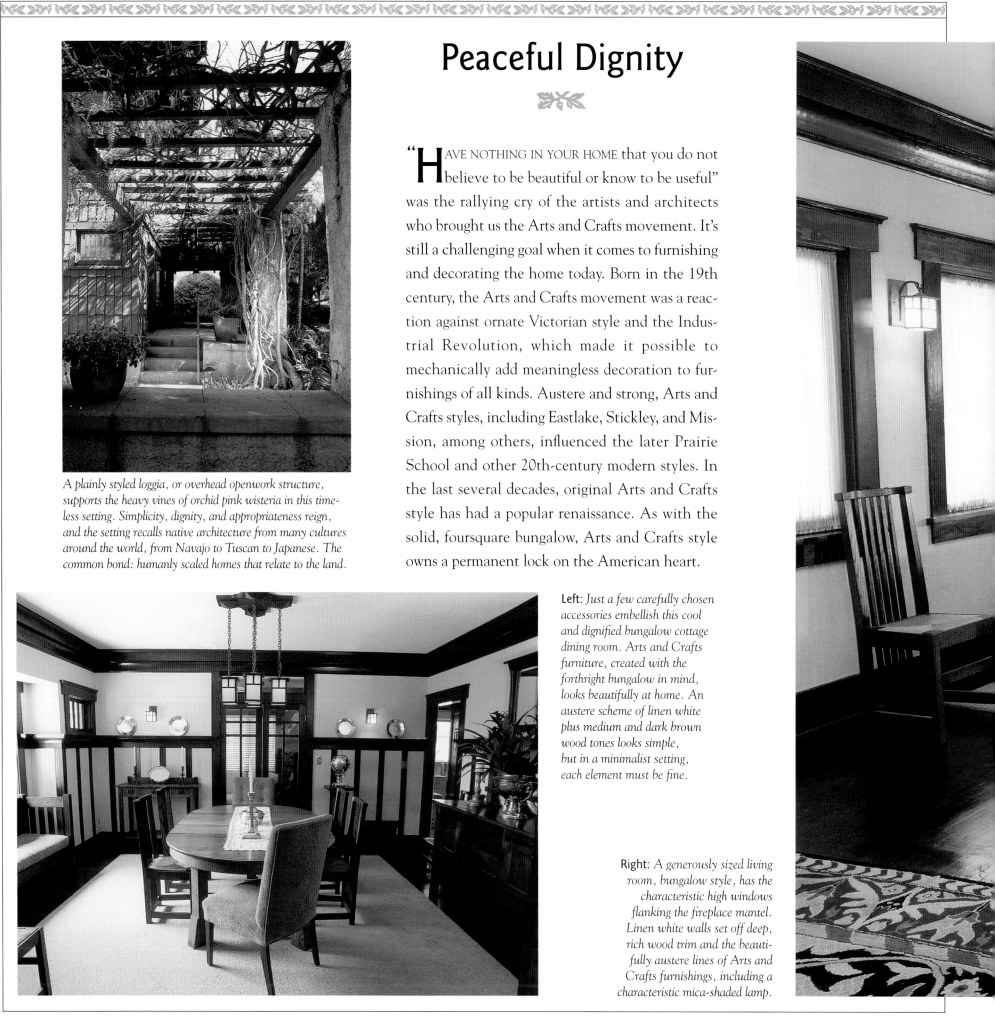

Right: *A generously sized living room, bungalow style, has the characteristic high windows flanking the fireplace mantel. Linen white walls set off deep, rich wood trim and the beautifully austere lines of Arts and Crafts furnishings, including a characteristic mica-shaded lamp.*

An old stove provides extra cooking and heating for this Shaker-inspired
home while offering a great design focal point for the kitchen. Decorative
detailing, like the tiny stenciled ducks parading around the room's perimeter,
adds charm without detracting from the essential simplicity.

O, Pioneers!

WHILE NOT EVERYONE can have a peaceful view of a woodland lake, it's distinctly possible to create a serene and simple retreat in the home you have. It just takes a bit of pioneering spirit and willingness to reject the usual solutions to home decorating. The first step to achieving this pioneer-inspired style: Just say no to mounds of trendy, landfill-destined accents. Instead, say yes to well-made essentials with a simple beauty of their own. Natural woods like knotty pine, lustrous maple, rich cherry, and interestingly grained oak contain surprising variety in themselves. Add a few painted and stenciled wood accents and simple, sturdy fabrics, and the job's almost done. It may take a bit of discipline to get used to this fairly austere style, but if the philosophy of living with fewer, better things appeals to you, why not go for it?

Russet red wall paint teamed with ivory white is a vintage combination that's stood the test of time. These colors give the wood furniture in the room a rich, warm tone and set off colorful fabrics brilliantly.
Architect: Centerbrook
Architects & Planners.

Sunset by a lakeshore in the woods: A more perfect prescription for serenity would be hard to imagine, almost any time of year. A few low-cost director's chairs are easy to tote out onto the deck to catch the day's last show.

Warm and Woodsy

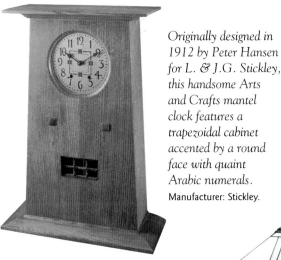

Originally designed in 1912 by Peter Hansen for L. & J.G. Stickley, this handsome Arts and Crafts mantel clock features a trapezoidal cabinet accented by a round face with quaint Arabic numerals. Manufacturer: Stickley.

W HEN YOU WANT to escape today's high-tech, sometimes chilly world, you can't get any further away than a rustic cottage. Here, the metal is wrought iron or antique brass—not shiny aluminum. The fabrics are cozy textured Native American blankets and soft old checked gingham and flannel—not slick synthetics. If you have a log home, you're halfway there, but if not, opt for log or peeled wood furniture. Seek out upholstered pieces that would work on the porch, such as settees, gliders, and rockers with lots of exposed wood. Choose fabrics with a warm texture and natural or jewel-tone colors: cranberry, hunter green, antique ivory, blue-green, russet, and old gold. For decorative accessories, keep that natural feeling: Mica lamp shades, accents depicting acorns and leaves, and other hallmarks of Arts and Crafts style will give a mellow glow to your rustic room.

Point blankets were introduced more than 200 years ago for trade with Native Americans. Each short line or "point" woven into the edge represented the number of beaver pelts to be exchanged for the blanket. Point blankets remain a valuable item—especially in rustic-style spaces where warmth and durability are the keys to comfort. Blanket: L.L. Bean Inc.

The bun feet and roll arms are traditional, but this wicker settee is anything but straitlaced. With sumptuous curves and overstuffed cushions, its tropical flair is a standout. Settee: Laura Ashley Home. Manufacturer: Whitecraft Rattan Inc.

Geometrically patterned leaded and stained glass; natural linen; and mica, a translucent, natural shell-like material in amber tones, were all favored for lamp shades by Arts and Crafts– and Mission-style designers. Manufacturer: Stickley.

Sometimes you want a lamp to really stand out; sometimes you just want it to do the job with a bit of quiet style. Black wrought iron can look rustic, modern, romantic, or classical, and this lamp enjoys a bit of all these inspirations. A plain white parchment "coolie hat" shade enhances the timeless simplicity. Manufacturer: Papila Design Inc.

Breezy and good-looking, this comfortable lounge chair and ottoman provide great transitional style for any sun porch or summer home setting. The wide braided border adds extra panache. Designer: Peter Rocchia. Manufacturer: The Wicker Works.

This Mission-style bed is made of oak and features the slatted headboard and footboard characteristic of the breed. What's special is the delicate inlay work depicting stylized lotus flowers in classic Arts and Crafts style. Manufacturer: Stickley.

In reaction to Victoriana's flowery bouquets, the Arts and Crafts designers favored pine-cones, acorns, and oak leaves as decorative motifs. This subtly colored rug features all of these in an appealing composition. Manufacturer: Whispering Pines.

Old World Charm

INFUSED WITH HISTORY and inspired by fairy tales, Old World cottage style has a magical appeal. Signature pieces in this style know all about growing old gracefully: copper and brass pots gone verdigris green, faded jewel-tone tapestry fabrics, mirrors with precious 24-karat gilding worn off by time, and ancient ceramic pots chipped and crazed but filled with character. Drawn mostly from romantic images of England and Europe, Old World cottage style embraces a wide range of looks. If you love flower gardens, English cot-

Staffordshire dogs have been a mainstay of English country style for several hundred years, often taking pride of place on the mantel, perhaps beneath an oil painting of beautiful hunting hounds. Dogs: Howards of Aberystwyth.

tage may speak personally to you with a subtle sage and tea rose palette. If hospitality is your middle name, Tuscan or French cottage style may be right for you, where terra cotta reigns along with richly colored print fabrics, copper pots, and crisp white cutwork curtains. Lighthearted Scandinavian cottage style pairs butter yellow with white and cobalt blue, a timeless scheme softened with curvy furniture painted white and warmed with accents of cheery red. Whatever look speaks your language, Old World cottage style says time is on your side.

Opulent, confident, and totally romantic, this English country–style room may be small in size, but it's big on charm and style. Pretty, vivid garden colors; floral images; elegant stripes; and pastoral paintings add up to a gracious mood that's both cozy and elegant. Designer: Beverly Ellsley, Beverly Ellsley Interiors.

Colorful Elegance

TRADITIONAL STYLE takes beautifully to expressive, confident color, as you can see from these rooms. European homes, whether a château or a cottage, often make use of more courageous color combinations than do American abodes, but done right, there's little risk. A traditional room treated to big color can be lively and elegant at the same time, like a vivacious hostess. To get the look, choose an untraditional color scheme and follow it through, making sure the colors appear at least three places in the room. Or, try a traditional color combination but punch up the colors to a dramatic level. In either of these decorating plans, traditionally styled furniture—in these rooms, classic 18th-century-style pieces—provide the stabilizing effect. The colors are free to take off and create an aura of excitement. Ornate molding painted bright white enhances the rooms' traditional elegance—and gives even more zip to the lively colors.

Gracious Living

THIS LATE 19TH-CENTURY HOME was brought up to speed with interior renovations and a large addition on the rear. But this is one house where new and old are integrated beautifully. The addition includes a new breakfast room (shown) plus a new family room, kitchen, and master suite. A rather formal decorating style recalls the stately European-furnished "cottages" of Newport and other seaside vacation towns of the same era, but you don't need to be near water to create this inviting look. Sherbet colors plus lots of white jump-start the lighthearted mood. That mood is enhanced by furniture with an abundance of rounded corners, curves, and bow fronts. Romantic 18th-century European influences appear in the English country–style living room and French-inspired breakfast room. The overall effect is pretty and graceful yet very livable.

Opposite: *A sunroom/porch on the front of the house is treated just as lovingly as the newer addition to the rear. White wicker furniture recalls the home's origins as a beach house; an artful mix of peach, cantaloupe, and green fabrics is pretty and inviting.* Architect: McKee Patterson, Austin Patterson Disston Architects, LLC.

Above: *A parlor-size living room doesn't have to work so hard thanks to the big new family room, but there's still a place for a cozy, pretty gathering spot like this. The teal green and apricot color scheme relates to the tones in the adjacent sun porch.*

Left: *This delightful breakfast room owes its charm in part to its octagonal shape and to the formal yet very pretty table and chairs. The room's unique shape makes for coziness inside and, from the exterior, helps break up the mass of a large addition.*

Black toile, stripes, checks, and florals give these romantic traditional rooms a fresh energy and sophistication. Walls of rich yellow cast a sunset glow onto the beautiful wood furniture and make black an especially snappy standout.

Pure Refinement

Opposite: *This is English country style at its most inviting. An artful mix of patterns—mostly large-scale florals and self-patterned solids—creates a traditionally comfortable look. Richly colored walls with fresh white trim set off dark cherry, mahogany, and walnut furniture.*

WHAT MAKES ENGLISH COUNTRY STYLE so appealing? Perhaps it's the air of relaxed refinement that seems an antidote to our busy, not always elegant daily lives. English style evolved in an often gray climate, and today it offers welcome relief for a modern world that's mostly gray concrete. This style embraces nature but in a romantic, whimsical way that has nothing to do with roughing it. (What else would you expect from the country that gave us Peter Rabbit and Peter Pan?) At the same time, English country style knows its roots and draws on a thousand years of dramatic history to keep the look from becoming too flowery. The tension between dignity and whimsy may have something to do with the charm of this English-style cottage. It all starts with handsome furniture in lustrous dark woods, richly colored walls sparked with white trim, and flowers. Lots of flowers!

Victorian Lite

Even the smallest bedroom can have a charming air if it's furnished in coddling Victorian style. Black wrought iron and dark antique wood play off enticingly against pretty bedding embellished with flowers and lace. What could be simpler?

ENGLAND'S QUEEN VICTORIA reigned throughout most of the 19th century, a period when, it was said, the sun never set on the British Empire. Happily married to Prince Albert, Victoria's reputation for priggishness was based on her passion for domestic bliss, an ideal that never really goes out of style. In recent decades, the success of Laura Ashley, Jessica McClintock, Ralph Lauren, and a host of other mega-designers shows the perennial popularity of Victorian style. But today's version has lost the fussiness and kept the sentimentality. We've said farewell to rooms full of dust-catching clutter and dark, gloomy colors but kept the curvy lines, the lace, and the coziness. Personal treasures and heirloom pieces get the visual breathing room they need from pale, simple backgrounds—and a few fearless touches, as shown here. Lightened up for modern taste, Victorian style still provides the same sentimental refuge it did over a hundred years ago.

Opposite: Washed in subtle gray-lilac, the walls of this room give an interesting dimension to a handsome scheme of black, white, and natural wood tones. Fine traditional furniture and offhand, whimsical accents—especially the spirited window treatments and the chandelier—mix it up in a distinctly modern way.

If you love Victorian style, you're in good company, which is why pretty pedestal sinks and claw-foot bathtubs like these are easy to find, even at home improvement stores. Raid the attic or a resale shop for handsome old wood storage pieces small enough for your bath.

Ravishing in Red

T HESE TWO ROOMS vividly illustrate the emotional power of red in a decorating scheme. In one room, the rosy tones are confined to the upholstery; in the other, the walls as well as the major upholstered pieces are swaddled in ruby tones. In both rooms, however, red clearly plays the leading role. Use red to draw attention to a special piece in the space, such as a really comfortable sofa with inviting lines or a fireplace wall embellished with a gilt-framed mirror. If the rest of the major elements in the setting are pale or neutral colors, the power of red will be even more apparent. (Do be sure, however, to add smaller red accents in several other places in the room.) If you're really smitten with the power of red, use it on walls as well as furniture to surround the space in friendly, seductive warmth. Either way, you'll have a setting that's rich and memorable.

A leaf green and white room has a fresh, timelessly elegant look, but it's the red upholstered pieces that really bring the space to life. A deft mix of a large-scale floral, a small-scale print, and a damask solid gives variety and interest to the shared crimson tones. Designer: Mary Ellen Mitchell, Mitchell Designs. Rug: Stark.

Opposite: *Ruby walls and a velvety red sofa give this room a wonderfully warm, luxurious air. Anyone would feel welcome in this hospitable space. The bright white trim and handsome ceiling further dramatize the rich red tones. The colors in the Oriental rug tie it all together.* Designer: Mary Ellen Mitchell, Mitchell Designs. Rug: Stark.

Chef's Special

IN OLDEN TIMES, kitchens were furnished like other rooms with whatever pieces the owner felt could be put to good use for various food preparation tasks. It took ages for the average homeowner to attain a kitchen where everything fit together and matched. But English architect and designer Johnny Grey lost no time in winning hearts with his "unfitted" kitchens that cleverly update the earlier unmatched approach—a look that goes perfectly with casual cottage style. Today's unfitted kitchens feature paintbox-bright colors and ergonomically specific kitchen surfaces. For example, you might want a prep counter at a comfortable lower height with a marble top for pastry-making. In these savvy spaces, heart-of-the-action kitchen islands and perching points for friendly guests put the "fun" in "functional."

An old-fashioned wall rack for plates is high style once again in today's unfitted kitchen. Colorfully painted cabinetry is decorated with iconographic symbols instead of the more expected stencils. A practical island with an inset granite work surface and a lower storage rack takes center stage.

Above: *An enormous commercial-style range is kept from dominating the room thanks to its soft and stylish bisque color. Above a granite backsplash with its own built-in spice shelf, ceramic tiles in a range of tawny golds make an appropriately warm design statement.*

Opposite: *Modern convenience meets timeless warmth in this appealing kitchen where nothing matches but everything works in concert. Standout features include a whimsically decorated cupboard and a large two-tiered kitchen island.* Designer: Johnny Grey, Johnny Grey, Inc.

Right: *An oddly sited fireplace looks nicely balanced thanks to the dramatic wall art above it. Tucked into the corner, a diminutive dressing table takes advantage of the nearby natural light. Taking center stage, a glorious jewel-tone velvet patchwork bedspread adds to the cozy, romantic ambience.*

Left: *An elephant on the mantel, an ancient figure near the hearth, a tribal mask on the armoire: These elements go far beyond the usual decorative accessories to create a mood of adventure and romance. An elaborately carved mirror provides a captivating focal point, and, if the ruby red antique carpet isn't magic, it sure looks like it could be.*

Rich with History

THIS ENGLISH COTTAGE is filled with quirky but gorgeous furniture, jewel-tone fabrics, meaningful art, and personal memories. The layering of elements reflects the layering of years that has gone into making this home what it is today. A big part of the mystique? The wealth of elements from India, Egypt, and other Eastern realms, perhaps souvenirs of an old soldier or a traveler in the empire of Victoria's England. Elaborately carved dark wood furniture, artifacts depicting ancient gods or tropical animals, and captivating mirrors and accents of all description create an irresistible, rather mysterious effect. These special elements reflect the dramatic influences of cultures that were part of the British Empire a century and a half before the concept of global design existed. Fortunately, it's an influence designers everywhere appreciate today. Scores of U.S. retailers are selling Eastern imports, from porcelain to silk hangings to mahogany furniture. Hunt for a few special pieces to make your rooms extraordinary.

English Garden Glories

IF YOU REALLY, truly, madly love a color, why not indulge yourself in it? This homeowner clearly adores brilliant fuchsia and other tones of red-violet, and its vibrant hues appear throughout the home. Savvy decorating has made this hot, stereotypically feminine color very livable in every room—proof that there are no difficult colors if they're handled with flair. The design started with an exuberant print fabric of deep pink parrot tulips on a buttercream yellow ground. The resultant scheme of fuchsia, yellow, green, and white is as fresh and delightful as a sun-drenched garden. Varying the proportions of the colors from room to room keeps the intense hues under control. In the living room, for example, white dominates, and the other three colors play supporting roles. In the dining room, fuchsia plays full out, but it's softened by abundant white and yellow. Give it a try with a few of your favorite colors for a scheme that's really "you."

Above: *Glorious fuchsia walls make a ravishing statement in this small dining room. The Queen Anne dining group might look bland in a white room, but here, surrounded in deep pink and rich golden yellow, the fine cherry wood tones fairly glow. Large white-curtained windows add cool balance to the hot-colored walls.* **Right:** *Green majolica plates make a unique decorating statement over the fireplace in this spacious room. White walls set off the pleasing lines of the slipper chairs, the sofa, and the French-inspired armchairs near the window. Accent colors of fuchsia, yellow, and green give the room a bright, hospitable feeling.* Interior designer: Lorraine Curley Interiors. Stylist: Joetta Moulden.

Warm, rosy tones in a medley of old-fashioned prints and patterns make this curvaceous bed even more inviting. The vintage rug adds another warm touch in the same color scheme. A simple bookcase keeps a lovingly collected array of personal mementos close at hand so the owner can enjoy them every day.

Set in Stone

A STONE-WALLED COTTAGE makes a romantic hideaway that's hard to resist. Making this home even more inviting, its owners have filled it with soft textures and appealing colors. Each room carries out a peaceful scheme of subtle gray, soft blue, and warm rose expressed in a nostalgic array of vintage fabrics. Thick wool rugs in a variety of antique styles add warmth and color underfoot, but it's the antique furniture that really stands out. Victorian for the most part, the furniture's curvy, rounded lines are wonderfully inviting. (Don't underestimate the psychological value of warm colors and rounded lines in creating a comfortable atmosphere. People will respond even if they can't identify the specific elements that make a room feel right.) If you don't have a real stone cottage, faux pierre, or false stone, wall treatments are a popular trompe l'oeil look. You may even be able to find it in stencils.

Opposite: Gray, raspberry, and cadet blue make a soothing scheme in this stone cottage parlor. Everything you need for comfort is right here: cushy chairs, a put-your-feet-up ottoman, a large no-nonsense coffee table, and a sofa long enough for a snooze. Small chairs holding plants and books strike a whimsical note. Interior designer: Janie Atwell Designs. Stylist: Joetta Moulden.

Designed to Delight

Yellow and orchid make a pretty, complementary color scheme that gives a spring-time air to this cottage-style bedroom. The charming mix of quilting patterns, gingham plaids, and floral chintz adds to the English country–style charm.

THE OWNER OF THIS HOME clearly loves yellow, and that cheerful tint appears in various guises throughout the house. In the bedroom, yellow is paired with orchid; in the living room/parlor and dining room, it's complemented by crimson. Throughout, shots of bright white give each room an even more lighthearted air. A merry mix of traditional patterns, some elegant and some casual, evoke the best of English country style. You can build up this charmingly lay-ered look with ease. First, choose a scheme of two or three colors (not including neutrals). Disciplining your colors lets you layer more elements without creating a cluttered look. Then, look for signature pieces that say English country style: pretty porcelain; Oriental rugs; flowered chintz fab-rics; plump pillows; and a mix of wood furniture pieces, from rustic oak to elegant mahogany. If the result is both curl-up cozy and garden fresh, you've captured the look!

Gingham and floral chintz make a cheerful and very charming window treat-ment in this cozy cottage dining room. Red-and-white toile chair covers add a whimsical touch.

Right: A pretty cottage parlor is chock-full of beguiling colors, patterns, and eye-catching decora-tive accessories, but the effect is cozy, not jarring.
Designer: Kitty Starling, IADA, Incredible Interiors.

Timeless Romance

I F THERE'S ONE cottage style that can easily be called elegant, it's one that recalls the rich and eloquent heritage of all things European. Actually, Old World cottage style embraces many different looks, so there's something for just about everyone. English cottage style brings spring flowers and floral tones indoors with layers of mood-brightening fabrics and a wealth of pretty floral porcelain pieces. French cottages, most often Provençal, capture a sunny spirit with intense blue, yellow, and red print fabrics and copper cookware. Italian cottage style is hearty and colorful, with dazzling hand-painted tiles; Portugal and Spain have a similar warm and lively spirit that's surprisingly contemporary, with architecturally simple shapes and sun-catching white surfaces. Scandinavian cottage style features white-painted traditional furniture and crisp primary colors for a look that's lighthearted. Other European cottage styles use a richer, darker palette, but all feature a wealth of handcrafted designs that make everyday items special. So rediscover your heritage—or borrow one you love. It's the American way!

Right: Blue-and-white china, whether it's from China, Sweden, England, France, or wherever, is beloved the world over. Have fun mixing rustic stoneware and elegant porcelain—scenics and florals, plain and fancy. As long as all the pieces are blue and white, you can't go wrong, and your table will have that wonderful acquired-over-generations look. Plate: Lovers of Blue & White.

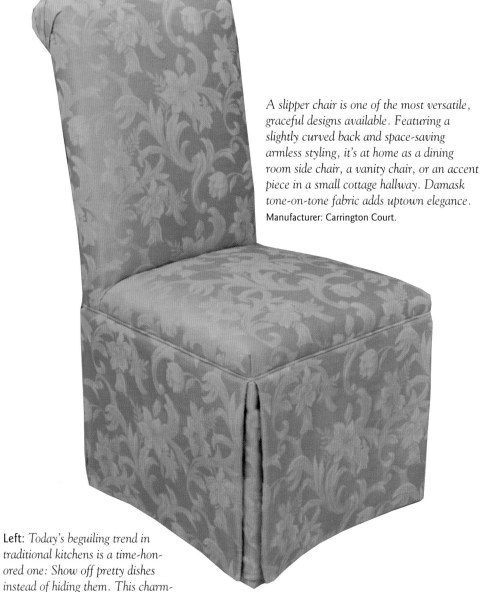

A slipper chair is one of the most versatile, graceful designs available. Featuring a slightly curved back and space-saving armless styling, it's at home as a dining room side chair, a vanity chair, or an accent piece in a small cottage hallway. Damask tone-on-tone fabric adds uptown elegance. Manufacturer: Carrington Court.

Left: Today's beguiling trend in traditional kitchens is a time-honored one: Show off pretty dishes instead of hiding them. This charming porte-assiette (plate rack) in distressed, painted pine is just the ticket. Plate rack: French Country Living.

Left: *Charmingly simple but with that certain je ne sais quoi, this Italian-made banquette was inspired by 19th-century benches along the Seine in Paris. The effect is downright sentimental and casual enough for today's lifestyles.* Bench: French Country Living.

Inspired by period furnishings found in villas on the Cote d'Azur, this fauteuil chair boasts the graceful lines of all things French. The cushions are surprisingly casual in ticking stripe fabric but lose nothing in the comfort department. Chair: French Country Living.

Park your laptop on something pretty, such as this beguiling French writing desk. Crackle finish in white gives an antique look; the dark leather top makes a nice cushion for handwriting love letters. Manufacturer: Lloyd Williams Furniture, Inc.

Garden Delights

ARDENING IS ONE OF America's best-loved pastimes, giving us a hands-on connection with the warmth and nurturance of the earth. But even if you don't have a green thumb, the simple beauty of cottage garden style will refresh your spirit any time. Unpretentious and pretty, the cottage garden look can flourish ten stories up as well as firmly on the ground. A white picket fence can surround your yard or serve as a whimsical headboard, and a faux-stone planter can hold geraniums and ivy near a sunny apartment window as well as on a rural porch. Wherever you are, bring in real outdoor furniture: wood; Victorian-style wrought iron; and vintage aluminum, such as springy 1940s chairs in Popsicle colors. Add fabrics in traditional floral or retro jungle prints. Look for wallcoverings with a lattice or trellis motif, or stencil flowering vines around windows. Stash everyday clutter in baskets and big faux-stone or terracotta pots, and add a touch of whimsy with a verdigris dragonfly or a porcelain frog. And don't forget a few easy-care flowering plants!

Above: A cast-iron urn with a pedestal base makes an impressive planter, indoors or out. If you'd like something easier to move around, you can find faux-iron models in lightweight aluminum. (If yours is real iron, be sure to protect floors from potential rust stains.) Urn: Smith & Hawken. Right: Wrought-iron and aluminum dining chairs with a dark green finish echo the curvy shapes of the wicker furniture pieces, while ample potted plants, including an ivy topiary as tall as a little tree, enhance the rather formal garden spirit of the space.

Easy Living

WHILE YOU CAN MAKE a charming statement with one or two vintage cottage accents, it's often more fun to carry the look further. In these homes, virtually every piece of furniture and every decorative accessory has a venerable history. Rather than taking a classically traditional approach, however, these homeowners chose elements that evoke casual country style, like the slatted coffee table or picket fence bench. Still other accessories verge on the quirky, like the bouncy old metal patio chairs on the porch. What they all have in common is the romantic patina of age. If you can't lay your hands on bona fide old treasures like these, why not give new unfinished furniture the distressed, crackled-paint effect you see here or shop for well-done reproductions of both furniture and fabrics? With millions of people in love with the garden cottage look, the elements to pull the look together are all around you.

Left: *Funky old 1940s-era porch chairs, a slatted table, and a comfy vintage glider couch are all you need for a wonderfully lazy afternoon. Even if you don't have the porch, the rest of the setting is well within reach. What's key: fabrics depicting tropical foliage in vintage 1930s and '40s styles.* **Opposite:** *This garden cottage room is filled with clever ideas. The child's chair hung on the wall to hold wildflowers is just the start. A white picket fence-turned-bench makes a comfortable perch piled with colorful cushions and pillows; timeworn painted wood chairs and tables offer easygoing hospitality.*

An Open Invitation

EVEN A SMALL ROOM can be comfortable and inviting if you make sure each piece serves a purpose. Using this philosophy, you can even indulge in larger pieces. Since you can fit in fewer of them, they actually make the room look less cluttered. Large-scale decorative accessories are a good idea, too: They'll look more important, and, of course, less stuff means less dusting! To further the no-fuss mood, adopt a cool, monochromatic color scheme like the one shown here. Green in a range of tints and tones looks friendly and soothing, especially when set off by white, tan, and other neutrals. What's especially interesting about this scheme is how fresh and contemporary it looks—proving garden cottage style can be chic enough to beguile even the most jaded city folk!

Opposite: *Traditional roll-arm furniture with charming ruffled skirts and simple plaid covers sets a farm-style mood in this cottage parlor. Instead of a muddle of small knickknacks, this room uses outsize accents for a fresh, contemporary update.*

As if the curvaceously charming bed weren't enough, this homeowner added a purely irresistible collection of real birds' nests to the scene. Wired to the simplest metal supports and entwined with faux ivy vines, the nests celebrate garden cottage style at its spontaneous best.

A spectacular view is a wonderful thing to have, but if you don't, take heart: Cover your table with layered checkered cloths, pull up a pair of rush-seat farm chairs, and set it all up beneath a conventional window filled with potted plants.

Right: *Rattan, wicker, or what have you: Natural woven furniture gives a slightly exotic look to any garden-inspired room. The tortoiseshell-colored bamboo shade underscores the room's scheme perfectly, and a medley of quiet neutrals creates a handsome, relaxing room.*

Quiet Sophistication

Glossy dark brown paint gives airy wicker chairs enough visual heft to hold their own with large cushy upholstered pieces. Because the room is quite narrow, the owners wisely painted the built-in storage unit and the brick fireplace pure white to visually expand the space.

GARDEN STYLE doesn't have to mean armfuls of pastel colors. If your taste runs toward a more sedate and soothing scheme, look beyond conventional floral tones and images. This cottage is swaddled in pale neutrals and earth tones, and the only flowers permanently on the scene are abstract ones on a few pillows and rugs. The garden inspiration is a subtle one, evoked largely by structural woody elements of the outdoors. Used together, wicker and rattan furniture and bamboo blinds create an airy, natural feeling. Against the creamy tones and earthen hues, a few hits of hot color have great impact without disturbing the peace. The best thing about building your room on a foundation of neutrals is that you can always add more colors, garden or otherwise, without having to invest in new major pieces. New wall paint and small accessories would give these rooms an entirely different feeling while preserving the soothing ambience.

Rich Impressions

THIS COTTAGE is cozy and pretty, but it's much more than that. It's filled with a wealth of precious family memories and treasures from the garden that make it truly one of a kind. Personal style doesn't get any more personal than this! A fearless but pleasing color scheme of deep blue-green and luscious red-violet adds contemporary passion and punch yet echoes the jewel-tone schemes beloved in the Victorian era. Strategic shots of white lighten up the whole scheme and add a special charm. If you didn't inherit a passel of old mahogany pieces from your grandmother, make a plan listing the pieces you need by function, then start hunting the flea markets and antique shops. And save a bit of room for that special little find: It's the things you love that make this look come alive.

Above: *Old handiwork and photos, lovingly framed on the wall and tabletop, create a vignette with great meaning for this homeowner. A Tiffany-style lamp, a pink Depression-glass candy dish, and a few other pretty finds add sparkle to the setting and underscore the cottage garden scheme of green, pink, and white.*

Left: *Upholstery in a dazzling magenta foulard pattern and teal moiré with burgundy stripes sets an exuberant, romantic air for this parlor-size cottage living room. Botanical wallpaper underscores the flower garden ambience, dark mahogany and oak furniture add substance, and garden statuary provides charming accents.*

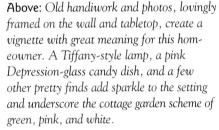

A scalloped dresser cloth, lace curtains, and an elaborate iron bed—all in pristine white—stand out beautifully against the deep teal green walls. A cozy boudoir like this is the perfect place to indulge a love of old family photos, pretty frames, and fresh-cut flowers.

Upscale and Inviting

A SOPHISTICATED TAKE on cottage style is apparent in every detail of this appealing space. French and English antiques certainly help create a romantic and elegant ambience, but there's more to it than that. A palette of pale colors is soothing to the eye and the spirit, and the simple, rather contemporary elements create a casual, relaxed feeling. Take the white windowpane-checked swags on the windows and the art over the fireplace: Heavy velvet draperies and a traditional still life painting would have a much more formal effect. Part of this room's charm is the abundance of rounded shapes in the room: small weathered-metal occasional tables, a comfortable but lightly scaled glass dining table, and the confection of a "pouf" ottoman. Gently rounded arches throughout the space further the soft, inviting mood. This is a place for retreat and reverie—but with great style and a sense of fun, too.

Right: *A glass-and-metal table designed for outdoor living makes a charming and practical indoor dining table. Antique chairs with cool cane backs and a distressed white-painted finish enhance the romantic, fresh look.*

Left: *Plump, inviting upholstered pieces; a delicate color scheme; and special touches of living greenery make for an elegant cottage environment. Simple window treatments add to the breezy feeling.* Designer: Susan Geier, ASID, Geier Goodman Design Associates, Inc.

Enchanted Forest

EVERYONE LOVES a fairy tale in which a boy and girl happen upon a cottage with a garden in the forest. These homeowners made that tale come true, but it didn't just happen. A lot of design savvy went into creating this little getaway. Outside, the line between natural and cultivated greenery is agreeably blurred with a simple garden surrounded by the woods. Open the door, and the line between inside and out is also a bit fuzzy, thanks to garden-inspired furnishings and faux finishes. To create a similar effect, look for lattice- or fence-motif stencils and wallpapers, use airy outdoor furniture, and accent with old gardening equipment such as wheelbarrows and potting stands. Terra-cotta pots; topiary forms; and, of course, lots of healthy green and flowering plants bring the look to life. Don't let things get too cute, but do indulge in a few whimsical touches. After all, this is a magical place.

Above: *Curvaceous wicker furniture beguiles now as it did in the Victorian era, especially in a dreamy teal-and-white finish. A floor hand painted in white-and-aqua checks enhances the airy garden ambience.*

This cottage set deep in the woods has so much style, a pair of formal stone lions looks just as at home as the casual rope hammock does. In a clearing, a simple sun-loving garden features rambling rose bushes, carefree daylilies, and a straw-covered floor to discourage weeds.

Opposite: *A narrow sleeping porch gets the romantic treatment from top to bottom, featuring a vine-covered chandelier set with electric candles over the foot of the iron bed and a hand-painted faux floor cloth below. A grand old painting and an antique wheelbarrow add contrasting darkness and depth.*
Designers: Ronnie and Kathy Owings.

The Great Indoors

Sunny yellow walls, evergreen storage shelves and potting tables, and an easygoing array of garden accoutrements make this room pretty and practical. If you don't have a potting shed or conservatory, a ground-floor laundry room or a corner of a sunroom may serve as a place to take care of your plants.

FLORAL FABRICS, botanical prints, leaf motifs, and pretty colors are a great start to garden style. But if you want to take it to the limit, use trompe l'oeil painting and real garden implements to bring the great outdoors inside. (If you can't find a local student artist to create your vision, send away for large-scale stencils depicting arbors, stone walls, and picket fences as well as plants.) The fun of this over-the-top approach is that it works its magic anywhere, even in a small apartment. If cutting down a few trees to make furniture isn't on your agenda, shop retailers of the Northwest lodge look for unpeeled cedar furniture. Or try the local patio shops: Romantic wrought iron and wicker, classic rattan and teak, and versatile aluminum furniture offer indoor furniture quality and outdoor flair. Accessorize with terra-cotta pots, watering cans, and the like. Then, stop and smell the roses.

Trompe l'oeil paints a winding stone pathway on the floor and coaxes faux sunflowers and hollyhocks to grow up the walls. In a room like this, bedposts made from real saplings seem perfectly logical. Patio furniture in wrought iron is a charming and practical touch. Designers: Jim Lord and Bobby Dent, Comfort Common.

A Mellow Point of View

THERE'S MORE THAN ONE WAY to create a relaxed, garden-inspired cottage room, as this space clearly shows. While the predictable springtime palette of blues, greens, and pinks plus white is certainly lovely, this room seems inspired by a more mellow season. Here, the strong gold and dramatic purple tones of late summer blooms hold court. A deft mix of modern upholstered pieces and antique furniture finds gives a look that's casual yet very sophisticated and aware. Because freshness is paramount in garden cottage style, all these rich tones are set off by lots of white. If you have a dark-paneled family room or recreation room, consider whitewash for the paneling to lighten things up, or simply bleach the wood for a brighter look. Be sure to carry the light look up onto any exposed ceiling beams. Bring in a few of your favorite garden colors, and watch your room come into bloom.

Above: *Modern and rustic meet happily in upholstery that combines nubby and shiny-smooth textures. In homage to the garden spirit, a pastoral painting and live ivy in pots make a simple but effective statement.*

Left: *Golden yellow, beige, and eggplant purple make a unique and very attractive scheme in this savvy living room. Plaid draperies and paisley-covered cushions unite all the colors in a modern yet comfortable way.* Designer: Mark Polo, Polo M.A., Inc. **Right:** *Deep aubergine purple is an unusual color for a garden-inspired room, but cut with gold and white, it's a handsome choice. The many-paneled screen, hand stenciled with garlands, makes a great backdrop.*

Right: Step into this beguiling parlor that's prim and pretty but not a bit prissy. A collection of pretty plates takes center stage, and a toile coffee table adds a punchy black accent. Slipper chairs in jewel-tone plaid and a drapery-free window add tailored touches that balance all the ornate floral elements in the room.

Making the most of a small sink area, this utterly romantic one-of-a-kind kitchen features a unique soffit-height mural inspired by medieval illustrations. A greenhouse window fitted with shelves shows off fun farmyard collections and thriving potted herbs. A mix of green tiles is another artistic touch that sets this special room apart.

Romance of the Rose

LUSCIOUS ROSE RED, cool celadon, soft greens, and white make a welcoming atmosphere for a pretty, garden-style cottage. As with any scheme based on complementary warm and cool colors, this cottage feels cozy and fresh at the same time. Within this scheme, every detail is created to enchant the eye—and other senses—with delight, making guests and family want to linger for hours. Part of the charm is contrasting textures: velvety chenille throws against crisp cotton chintz upholstery, gleaming porcelain treasures against weathered wood. But the rooms aren't just jumbles of various elements. Each has a special focal point around which the rest of the space is organized. For example, one room highlights an ornate old mirror surrounded by plates, another features a window seat overlooking a rose garden, and the third draws the eye with a spectacular medieval-inspired mural. This is clearly a cottage for happily ever afters.

Cabana stripes in pretty celadon and white are wonderfully fresh and inviting in this narrow dining room. They also draw attention to the spacious window seat, a cottage must-have. Rustic and delicate elements combine prettily thanks to a harmonious rose, green, and white color scheme.

Fresh-picked Charm

CITY MOUSE or country mouse, if you love the look of garden style, you can easily find elements to bring it all home. People everywhere crave the quiet optimism and creativity a garden evokes, but you don't need a green thumb to pick today's crop of garden-inspired furnishings. Beds with white picket fence headboards; round metal tables that seem plucked from outdoor cafés; and lightweight, large-scale planters with the look of weathered stone garden ornaments are easy to find, along with the many other pieces that owe their origins to the garden. In particular, the casual and outdoor furniture stores offer a great array of pieces. You can choose from wicker and rattan (the real thing or all-weather versions), wrought iron, lightweight aluminum, and weather-resistant teak or treated pine. Flowers remain one of the most popular fabric motifs, so it's easy to find upholstery, window treatments, and throw pillows to suit any decorating scheme. Add a few live plants, and enjoy the view.

Left: *An étagère with copper trays elevates even ordinary potted plants to exotic garden style. One like this can be staked in the ground or bolted to a deck. Étagères, like baker's racks, are very popular, so you can also find conventionally footed ones for use as indoor furniture.* Étagère: Smith & Hawken.

Sinuously shaped, this chaise lounge is the star of any sunroom with its chic, fresh look. The natural woven frame is made of water hyacinth reeds, and its moderne-style feet are teak. Lounge: Smith & Hawken.

Above: *Like a find from Cinderella's attic, this mirror with its decorative, handcrafted iron flowers introduces a whimsical approach to grooming. Whether vintage 1940s finds or new reproductions, this is a fun, glamorous look in lighting fixtures as well as mirrors.* Mirror: Ballard Designs.

White wicker works in almost any cottage or vacation home setting, but it's especially winsome in a garden-inspired space. Treated with high-gloss paint, durable synthetic wicker looks like the real thing and is a practical choice for outdoor use. Swing: Plow & Hearth.

Above: A French-inspired clock decorated with tiny fleur de lis and vintage-style roses adds a fun and practical accent to your garden room. Clock: Ballard Designs. **Below:** An airy daybed is a romantic touch for any sunroom. This vintage style is French-inspired, handwrought in iron, and finished for an aged look. Daybed: Ballard Designs.

A pretty little stool like this always comes in handy. This one is neoclassically inspired, with a hand-stitched wool needlepoint seat and brass nailhead trim. Stool: Ballard Designs.

Resource Directory

ARCHITECTS

Austin Patterson Disston Architects, LLC
376 Pequot Ave.
P.O. Box 61
Southport, CT 06490
phone 203-255-4031
info@apdarchitects.com
www.apdarchitects.com
McKee Patterson
(84, 85)

Bernhard & Priestley Architecture LLC
22 Central St.
Rockport, ME 04856
phone 207-236-7745
(56, 57)

Centerbrook Architects & Planners
67 Main St.
P.O. Box 955
Centerbrook, CT 06409
phone 860-767-0175
(76, 77)

Thayer Hopkins
1129 Kansas St.
San Francisco, CA 94107
phone 415-434-0320
fax 415-434-2409
thayer.hopkins@fme-arch.com
(28)

Mark Hutker & Associates
P.O. Box 820
West Fairmouth, MA 02574
phone 508-693-3344
fax 508-693-8776
mhaa@capeonramp.com
(26, 27)

Stephen Blatt Architects
10 Danforth St.
Portland, ME 04101
phone 207-761-5911
fax 207-761-2105
sjb@sbarchitects.com
Stephen Blatt
(54)

BUILDERS

Bob Moore Construction
P.O. Box 2075
Jackson, WY 83001
phone 307-733-4971
fax 307-739-2411
(62, 63)

Castlerock Homes Inc.
347 N.W. 83rd Pl.
Portland, OR 97229
phone 503-292-2819
fax 503-292-1340
casrock7@aol.com
(68, 69)

Rocky Mountain Log Homes
1833 Highway 93 S
Hamilton, MT 59840
phone 406-363-5680
fax 406-363-2109
sales@rmlh.com
www.rmlh.com
(6, 70, 71)

DESIGNERS

Alex Anderson
1558 De Soto Way
Livermore, CA 94550
phone 925-447-6679
fax 925-454-1080
alexandrsn@aol.com
(52)

Ann Platz & Co.
1266 W. Paces Ferry Road
Suite 521
Atlanta, GA 30327
phone 404-237-1000
fax 404-237-3810
annplatz@flash.net
www.annplatz.com
Ann Platz
(34, 35, 40, 41, 58, 59)

Beverly Ellsley Interiors
179 Post Road W
Westport, CT 06880
phone 203-227-1157
Beverly Ellsley
(80–81)

Comfort Common
717 High St.
Comfort, TX 78013
phone 830-995-3030
Jim Lord and Bobby Dent
(118, 119)

Duffy's Designs Inc.
215 S. Highway 101
Suite 102
Solana Beach, CA 92075
phone 858-481-3449
fax 858-481-3386
lynnduffys@aol.com
Lynn Crosby Harland, ASID
(14, 15)

Geier Goodman Design Associates, Inc.
162 S. Rancho Santa Fe Road
Suite A55
Encinitas, CA 92024
phone 760-753-6649
fax 760-753-0374
Susan Geier, ASID
(114, 115)

Harvestings
254 Cave Creek Road
Fredericksburg, TX 78624
fax 830-990-8288
wwhite@ktc.com
(50, 51)

Mike and Meri Hern
The Hilltop Inn
Main St.
Sugar Hill, NH 03585
phone 800-770-5695
(33)

Incredible Interiors
327 Seminole Dr.
Marietta, GA 30060
phone 770-794-6620
fax 770-794-1972
kitstar@mindspring.com
Kitty Starling, IADA
(contents, 100, 101)

Janie Atwell Designs
Home Sweet Home
Fredericksburg, TX 78624
phone 830-669-2474
(98, 99)

Jayne Sanders Interior Design
215 W. 37th St.
Vancouver, WA 98660
phone 360-695-2279
fax 360-694-2720
(68, 69)

Johnny Grey, Inc.
101 Henry Adams St., Suite 424
San Francisco, CA 94103
phone 415-701-7701
fax 415-701-7702
johnny@johnnygrey.com
www.johnnygrey.com
Johnny Grey
(92, 93)

Lorraine Curley Interiors
141 Arden Road
Columbus, OH 43214
phone 614-447-0500
(96, 97)

Mascord Design Associates
1305 N.W. 18th Ave.
Portland, OR 97229
phone 503-225-9161
fax 503-225-0933
www.mascord.com
(68, 69)

Mitchell Designs
8055 Fairfax Road
Alexandria, VA 22308
phone 703-660-9511
fax 703-660-8623
mmitchelldesigns@aol.com
Mary Ellen Mitchell
(82, 83, 90, 91)

Motif Designs
20 Jones St.
New Rochelle, NY 10801
phone 914-633-1170
Lyn Peterson
(30–31, 49)

Joetta Moulden
9337-B Katy Freeway #176
Houston, TX 77024
phone 713-461-2063
www.shelterstyle.com
(96, 97, 98, 99)

Ronnie and Kathy Owings
515 Cotton Indian Creek
McDonough, GA 30252
phone 770-914-9554
(116, 117)

Polo M.A., Inc.
1107 Buckingham Road
Fort Lee, NJ 07024
phone 201-224-0322
Mark Polo
(120, 121)

Luciana Samu
P.O. Box 165
Bayport, NY 11715
(16, 17)

Silver Sage Design
P.O. Box 7464
Jackson, WY 83002
phone 307-733-4318
fax 307-733-4032
daren@silversagedesign.com
www.silversagedesign.com
Daren Martin Walsh, ASID
(62, 63)

Simple Slips
1306 N. Llano St.
Fredricksburg, TX 78624
phone 830-990-0616
(42, 43)

MANUFACTURERS

Carrington Court
P.O. Box 600
Hickory, NC 28603
phone 828-396-1049
fax 828-256-4854
info@carringtoncourtdirect.com
www.carringtoncourtdirect.com
(102)

Ficks Reed
6245 Creek Road
Cincinnati, OH 45242
phone 513-985-0606
fax 513-985-9293
ficksreed@aol.com
www.ficksreed.com
(29)

Lexington Home Brands
P.O. Box 1008
Lexington, NC 27293
phone 336-249-5915
fax 336-249-5146
lharris@lexington.com
www.lexington.com
(7)

Lloyd Williams Furniture, Inc.
108 E. Diamond St.
Suite 105
Butler, PA 16001
phone 724-282-4990
fax 724-282-0558
info@lloydwilliams.com
www.lloydwilliams.com
(103)

Maine Cottage
P.O. Box 935
Yarmouth, ME 04096
phone 207-846-1430
fax 207-846-0602
info@mainecottage.com
www.mainecottage.com
(title page, contents, 8, 12, 13, 22, 23, 28, 29)

Papila Design Inc.
5505 Carder Road
Orlando, FL 32810
phone 407-293-0600
fax 407-293-1889
papiladesign@cs.com
www.papiladesign.com
(79)

Sanderson
Sanderson House
Oxford Road, Denham
UB9 4DX UNITED KINGDOM
phone 011-44-1895-830-044
fax 011-44-1895-830-055
cvc@a-sanderson.co.uk
www.sanderson-online.co.uk
(38)

Stark
Decoration & Design Building
979 Third Ave.
New York, NY 10022
phone 212-752-9000
(82, 83, 90, 91)

Stickley
Stickley Dr.
P.O. Box 480
Manlius, NY 13104-0480
phone 315-682-5500
fax 315-682-6306
www.stickley.com
(78, 79)

Swedish Blonde
Odinsvägen 37A
SE-130 54 Dalarö
SWEDEN
phone 011-46-8501-502-26
fax 011-46-8501-502-51
millang@avancee.se
www.swedish-blonde.com
(52)

The Wicker Works
1237 Minnesota St.
San Francisco, CA 94107
phone 415-970-5400
fax 415-970-5410
tom@thewickerworks.com
www.thewickerworks.com
(28, 79)

PHOTOGRAPHERS

Abode UK
Albion Ct.
1 Pierce St.
Macclesfield, Cheshire
SK11 6ER ENGLAND
phone 011-44-1625-500-070
fax 011-44-1625-500-910
(39, 94, 95)

Sandy Agrafiotis
548 Emery's Bridge Road
South Berwick, ME 03908
phone 207-676-2728

Alexander Vertikoff
    Photography
P.O. Box 2079
Tijeras, NM 87059
phone 505-281-7489
(60, 61)

Austin Bewsey Studio
4650 Wilmer Ave.
Cincinnati, OH 45226
phone 513-871-8660
fax 513-871-8692
austinbewseystudios@fuse.net
www.bewseystudios.com
(29)

Brad Simmons Photography
870 Craintown Road
Perryville, KY 40468
phone 859-332-8400
(front cover, 4, 32, 33, 36, 37, 42,
    43, 44, 45, 46, 47, 50, 51, 86, 87,
    88, 89, 96, 97, 98, 99, 106, 107,
    108, 109, 118, 119)

Brady Architectural Photography
1010 University Ave.
San Diego, CA 92103
phone 619-296-5304
fax 619-296-5304
Jim Brady
(14, 15, 114)

Adrianne dePolo
375 Forest Ave.
Rye, NY 10580
phone 914-967-9538
fax 914-967-9539
(84, 85)

John Hoover & Ed Vaugha
Gaithersburg, MD 20878
phone 301-814-1400 or
703-799-3030
(82, 83, 90, 91)

James Brown Photography
917 Summit Drive
South Pasadena, CA 91030
phone 323-254-7178
fax 323-259-0685
kingosoul@aol.com
Jim Brown
(74, 75)

Mark Lohman Photography
1021 S. Fairfax Ave.
Los Angeles, CA 90019
phone 323-933-3359
fax 310-471-6268
(back cover, 10, 11, 20, 21, 24, 25,
    110, 111, 122, 123)

McKinney Photography
180½ North Ave.
San Francisco, CA 94118
phone 415-752-4070
(104–105)

Colin McRae
2836 Tenth St.
Berkeley, CA 94710
phone 510-644-0180
fax 510-644-0219
colin@mcraephoto.com
(28, 79)

Melabee M. Miller Photography
29 Beechwood Pl.
Hillside, NJ 07205
phone 908-527-9121
fax 908-527-0242
(5, 6, 89)

Moreland Photography, Inc.
160 Roswell Farms Lane
Roswell, GA 30075
phone 770-993-6059
fax 770-998-7050
mmfoto@mindspring.com
www.morelandphoto.com
Mike Moreland
(contents, 100, 101)

David Papazian
P.O. Box 13146
Portland, OR 97213
phone 503-282-9208
(68, 69)

Phillip H. Ennis Photography
114 Millertown Road
Bedford, NY 10506
phone 914-234-9574
(30–31, 72, 73, 80–81, 120, 121)

PRO Studio
3825 Jodeco Road
McDonough, GA 30253
phone 678-432-1269
fax 678-423-1270
ronnie@prostudionet.com
Ronnie Owings
(34, 35, 40, 41, 58, 59 112, 113,
    116, 117)

Roger Wade Studio, Inc.
P.O. Box 1130
Condon, MT 59826
phone 406-754-2793
fax 406-754-3070
info@rogerwadestudio.com
www.rogerwadestudio.com
(70, 71)

Samu Studios
P.O. Box 165
Bay Port, NY 11705
phone 212-754-0415
www.samustudios.com
(16, 17)

Tony Sylvestro
phone 804-644-0348
(53, 102, 103)

Brian Vanden Brink
39 Curtis Ave.
Camden, ME 04843
phone 207-236-4035
(18, 19, 26, 27, 54, 56, 57, 64, 65,
    76, 77)

Stephanie P. von Ohain
Källtorpsvägen 3
SE-136 70 Haninge
SWEDEN
phone 011-46-8776-49-93
fax 011-46-8776-32-71
vonohain@yahoo.com
(52)

Dominique Vorillon
1636 Silverwood Terrace
Los Angeles, CA 90026
phone 323-660-5883
fax 323-660-5575
(8–9)

Wolff Images
1821 Industrial Drive
Wadena, MN 56482
phone 218-631-3522
Doug Wolff
(62, 63)

RETAILERS

Ballard Designs
1670 Defoor Ave.
Atlanta, GA 30318
phone 800-367-2775
www.ballarddesigns.com
(contents, 52, 53, 124, 125)

Della Vita
317 N.W. Gilman Blvd.
Suite 42
Issaquah, WA 98027
www.dellavita.net
(53)

French Country Living
5568 W. Chester Road
West Chester, OH 45069
phone 800-485-1302
fax 866-226-6796
www.frenchcountry.com
(53, 102, 103)

Howard of Aberystwyth
P.O. Box 149
Aberystwyth, Wales
UNITED KINGDOM SY23 1WQ
phone 011-44-1545-570-576
fax 011-44-1545-570-576
info@staffordshires.com
www.staffordshires.com
(80)

L.L. Bean Inc.
Freeport, ME 04033-0001
phone 800-441-5713
fax 207-552-3080
www.llbean.com/home
(78)

Laura Ashley Home
7000 Regent Parkway
Fort Mill, SC 29715
phone 800-463-8075
marketingna@lauraashley-usa.com
www.laura-ashleyusa.com
(29, 78)

Lovers of Blue & White
Steeple Morden
Royston, Hertfordshire
ENGLAND SG8 0RN
phone 011-44-1763-853-800
fax 011-44-1763-853-700
china@blueandwhite.com
www.blueandwhite.com
(102)

Plow & Hearth
P.O. Box 5000
Madison, VA 22727
phone 800-627-1712
fax 800-843-2509
info@plowhearth.com
www.plowhearth.com
(125)

Smith & Hawken
Corporate Offices
4 Hamilton Landing
Novato, CA 94949
phone 800-776-3336
www.smithandhawken.com
(contents, 30, 104, 124)

Spiegel
3500 Lacey Road
Downers Grove, IL 60515
phone 630-986-8800
fax 630-769-3686
www.spiegel.com
(39, 48, 49)

Whispering Pines
43 Ruane St.
Fairfield, CT 06430
phone 203-259-5027
(contents, 54, 66, 67, 79)

Whitecraft Rattan Inc.
7350 N.W. Miami Ct.
Miami, FL 33150
phone 305-757-8835
whitecraft@aol.com
www.whitecraft.com
(29, 78)

OTHER RESOURCES

Fuller Cottage Bed & Breakfast
229 Spring St.
Eureka Springs, AR 72632
phone 501-751-7766
(44, 45)

Photo Credits

Front cover: **Brad Simmons Photography**
Back cover: **Mark Lohman Photography**

Abode UK: 39, 94, 95; **Alexander Vertikoff Photography:** 60, 61; **Austin Patterson Disston Architects, LLC/Adrianne dePolo:** 84, 85; **Ballard Designs:** contents (right center), 52 (top), 53 (top right), 124 (right center), 125 (top left, bottom left & bottom right); **Brad Simmons Photography:** 4, 32, 33, 36, 37, 42, 43, 44, 45, 46, 47, 50, 51, 86, 87, 88, 89, 96, 97, 98, 99, 106, 107, 108, 109, 118, 119; **C & T Publishing Inc.:** 52 (bottom left); **Carrington Court:** 102 (bottom right); **Castlerock Homes Inc./David Papazian:** 68, 69; **Della Vita:** 53 (bottom left); **Duffy's Designs Inc./Brady Architectural Photography:** 14, 15; **Ficks Reed/Austin Bewsey Studio:** 29 (bottom); **French Country Living/Tony Sylvestro:** 53 (bottom right), 102 (bottom left), 103 (top left & right center); **Geier Goodman Design Associates, Inc.:** Brady Architectural Photography: 114; Ed Gohlich Photography: 115; **John Howard/Howard of Aberystwyth:** 80; **Incredible Interiors/Moreland Photography, Inc.:** contents, 100, 101; **James Brown Photography:** 74, 75; **Johnny Grey, Inc.:** 92, 93; **Laura Ashley Home Manufactured Under License by Whitecraft Rattan Inc.:** 29 (top center & top right), 78 (left center); **Lexington Home Brands:** 7; **L.L. Bean Inc.:** 78 (center); **Lloyd Williams Furniture, Inc.:** 103 (bottom left); **Lovers of Blue & White:** 102 (top); **Maine Cottage:** title page, contents, 8, 12, 13, 22, 23, 28 (bottom), 29 (top left); **Mark Lohman Photography:** 10, 11, 20, 21, 24, 25, 110, 111, 122, 123; **McKinney Photography:** 104–105; **Melabee M. Miller Photography:** 5, 6 (top), 89 (top); **Mitchell Designs/John Hoover & Ed Vaugha:** 82, 83, 90, 91; **Papila Design Inc.:** 79 (top left); **Phillip H. Ennis Photography:** 30–31, 72, 73, 80–81, 120, 121; **Plow & Hearth:** 125 (top right); **PRO Studio:** 112, 113, 116, 117; Ann Platz & Co.: 34, 35, 40, 41, 58, 59; **Rocky Mountain Log Homes:** 6 (bottom); **Roger Wade Studio, Inc.:** 70, 71; **Samu Studios:** 16, 17; Sanderson: 38; **Silver Sage Design/Wolff Images:** 62, 63; **Smith & Hawken:** contents, 30, 104, 124 (top & left center); **Spiegel:** 39, 48, 49; **Stickley:** 78 (top & right center), 79 (bottom left); **Swedish Blonde/Stephanie P. von Ohain:** 52 (bottom right); **Brian Vanden Brink:** 18, 19, 26, 27, 55, 56, 57, 64, 65, 76, 77; **Deborah VanKirk:** 53 (top left); **Dominique Vorillon:** 8–9; **Whispering Pines:** contents, 54, 66, 67, 79 (bottom right); **The Wicker Works/Colin McRae:** 28 (top), 79 (top right).